Business Without Boundaries

An Action Framework for Collaborating Across Time, Distance, Organization, and Culture

Don Mankin

Susan G. Cohen

JOSSEY-BASS
A Wiley Imprint
www.josseybass.com

Published by Jossey-Bass
A Wiley Imprint
989 Market Street, San Francisco, CA 94103-1741   www.josseybass.com

Jossey-Bass books and products are available through most bookstores. To contact Jossey-Bass directly call our Customer Care Department within the U.S. at 800-956-7739, outside the U.S. at 317-572-3986, or fax 317-572-4002.

Jossey-Bass also publishes its books in a variety of electronic formats. Some content that appears in print may not be available in electronic books.

Library of Congress Cataloging-in-Publication Data

Mankin, Donald A., 1942-
  Business without boundaries : an action framework for collaborating across time, distance, organization, and culture / by Don Mankin, Susan G. Cohen.—1st ed.
     p. cm.—(The Jossey-Bass business & management series)
  Includes bibliographical references and index.
  ISBN 0-7879-5911-1 (alk. paper)
  1. Strategic alliances (Business)—Case studies. 2. Interorganizational relations—Case studies. 3. Academic-industrial collaboration—Case studies. 4. International business enterprises—Case studies. I. Cohen, Susan G. II. Title. III. Series.
  HD69.S8.M3275 2004
  658'.044—dc22   2004015336

Printed in the United States of America

FIRST EDITION
HB Printing   10 9 8 7 6 5 4 3 2 1

The Jossey-Bass

Business & Management Series

Contents

*Don dedicates this book to his
best, closest, and favorite collaborators:
in life, his wife, Katherine;
in work, his coauthor, colleague,
and friend, Susan.*

*Susan dedicates this book to
her closest collaborators:
her husband, Steve;
her son, Danny;
and her coauthor, Don.*

Preface

To paraphrase the often quoted line from the Grateful Dead's signature song, this has been a long strange trip. We suppose that most books involve long and often strange "trips," but our trip has seemed longer and stranger than most. This book started out as something very different. It grew out of our long-term interest in collaboration as well as out of the long-term collaboration between the two of us.

The roots of our collaboration go back to 1989 and a meeting that took place not quite by chance at a conference in Boulder, Colorado. We liked each other, discovered common interests, and were soon collaborating on our first joint book, *Teams and Technology*, coauthored with Tora K. Bikson and published in 1996.

That collaboration went surprisingly well. The process of writing the book was hugely satisfying for both of us. We frequently marveled at how much we enjoyed working together and how smoothly our meetings went. Differences of opinion were expressed candidly but never contentiously, and we seemed to resolve those differences quickly. We always left our meetings feeling good about our work and feeling good about each other. We believe that the final product is a good indication of the success of our collaborative efforts.

When we weren't talking about the substance of our book, or of the several papers, proposals, and presentations that followed, we were talking about what it was that made our collaboration so fulfilling and effective (besides the fact that we share the same birthday—April 22, in case you're curious or want to send us presents). If we could figure out the secret of our successful collaboration, we thought, we would have the basis for a very interesting and useful book. Because one-to-one collaboration was of most interest to us, that is where we started. We began interviewing other collaborating pairs—not just our colleagues but also a successful screenwriting team (after all, we do live in Los Angeles).

It wasn't long before we realized that our particular focus was somewhat self-indulgent and might not be so interesting to those in the business world, who generally had to deal with collaborations that were far more complex. What was on the minds of the businesspeople we talked to were collaborations that involved not only one-to-one interactions like ours but also collaborations among different teams and organizations, often in very different parts of the world. Research on virtual teams conducted with Cristina Gibson, Arjan Raven, and Alec Levenson of the Center for Effective Organizations (CEO), put us in touch with several companies that were struggling to collaborate virtually and were looking for frameworks to help them manage the complexity. It soon became clear—from our discussions and this research, from feature articles and other pieces in the media, and from our thinking about what was happening in the world—that we were entering a new era of global collaboration.

As a result, we shifted our attention to these more complex collaborations and quickly found a new focus for our interests. We also realized that this new, higher-level focus did not preclude a more intimate focus on one-to-one collaboration but instead subsumed it. Complex collaborations include one-to-one interactions as well as collaborations at the next level of complexity: face-to-face interactions within intact work teams. But they also go well beyond that, to collaborations that cross all kinds of boundaries, including those of time, distance, organization, and culture.

Ultimately, we decided that the book we wanted to write would be about how to design, implement, and manage collaborations among dispersed teams, multiple organizations, and diverse cultures. Despite many challenges, our collaboration has more than survived—it has thrived. We are still trying to figure out what makes it work. Maybe it is our common birthday, and maybe we'll get to address that issue in our next book. In the meantime, we hope you enjoy reading this one as much we enjoyed writing it.

Many people have helped us get from there to here. Both of us would like to acknowledge those who helped us identify our three cases and get us in the door at those companies. Thanks to Karen Berman and Jan Chalupnik-Johnson for the John Deere case, to Jim O'Toole for the Radica case, and to Karie Willyerd for the Solectron case. We would also like to thank those who are mentioned as key figures in our case descriptions, especially Richard Park and Mick Sims at John Deere; Pat Feely at Radica, and Bob Davids and S. W. Lam, formerly at Radica; and David Moezidis at Solectron and Matt Taylor at Brocade, Solectron's supply-chain collaborator. Charley Grantham and Stacey Bressler were our first interviewees, when our focus was still on one-to-one collaboration. We thank them for their time, insights, and perspectives, which will be especially useful if we ever decide to revisit, in another book, the focus we originally had in mind.

We would also like to acknowledge three people who read an earlier, rougher, and much longer draft: Jan Klein, Mike Beyerlein, and an anonymous reviewer who didn't mince words in describing the earlier draft's flaws. The comments of all three helped us immeasurably in refining our focus and tightening the book. Mike deserves special thanks for the many stimulating conversations about teams and teamwork that we have had with him over the years. Susan Williams and Rob Brandt provided excellent editorial guidance throughout the project.

We are also very much indebted to Susan's colleagues at CEO, in the Marshall School of Business at the University of Southern California, who have stimulated our thinking over the years. We especially want to acknowledge Ed Lawler, who has created and led a center that promotes collaboration within and across its boundaries. Sue Mohrman has helped shape the way both of us view organizations; she has been not only a terrific colleague but also a good friend. Jim O'Toole deserves special thanks for directing us, in one of our early conversations about this book, away from a preliminary, less promising focus and toward our current emphasis. Ramón Rico, who visited CEO from the University of Madrid, influenced the way we thought about designing organizations for collaboration and has given us the opportunity to collaborate internationally. Other colleagues include Jay Conger, John Boudreau, and Alec Levenson at CEO, and Cristina Gibson, formerly at CEO; all of them have challenged us intellectually and provided support.

We would be remiss if we did not acknowledge the efforts of the CEO staff, who made this book a reality. Dan Canning helped us with graphics (only one of which we ultimately used, but that wasn't his fault). Ruth Perez insured that the manuscript's formatting was correct. A special acknowledgment goes to Annette Yakushi, who managed the process of producing the final manuscript and took care of whatever needed to be done whenever it needed to be done.

We also realize, as experienced collaborators, that our own collaboration is enhanced by the collaborations that each of us has with others. Numerous conversations over the years have helped us bring new ideas and information to each other.

Don Mankin's conversations have been (to mention just a few) with Dan Heitzer, Ken and Maddy Dychtwald, Frank Wuest, Robert Hogan, Catherine Sim, Norbert Tanzer, Susan Nero, Tom Rollins, Troy Jensen, and his former students, especially those in his spring 2003 seminar on complex collaborations, conducted at the former California School of Professional Psychology. Don would also like to thank the two women who made all of this possible: Katherine, his long-suffering and patient wife, who had to put up with a husband who grew more cranky and irascible as the project wore on;

and his collaborator, Susan Cohen, for sparking his interest in a new direction and showing him what courage and commitment are all about.

Susan Cohen extends a very special acknowledgment and thanks to her oncologist, Dr. James Waisman, and to her breast surgeon, Dr. Carey Cullinane, and their nurses and staff at Breastlink, in Torrance, California. This is the second book that Susan has completed while undergoing treatment for breast cancer. Originally diagnosed in February 2001, she has had three local recurrences and underwent surgery, chemotherapy, and radiation while this book was being written. Drs. Waisman and Cullinane and the Breastlink nurses and staff, through their exemplary teamwork and skills, have kept many patients alive over the years. Susan would also like to thank the women in the chemotherapy room, and her support group at the Wellness Community, who demonstrated personal courage and never ceased to provide emotional support despite their own trying circumstances. Susan's journey as a breast cancer survivor has taught her what emotional resilience and courage mean.

Finally, Susan would like to thank the one boy and two men who make the journey worthwhile and possible. Susan's son, Danny Lampert, is now six years old, and every day he lets his mom know what's really important. Susan's husband, Stephen Lampert, has been there for her through thick and thin, and she feels lucky to have him as her husband. And Susan cannot find the words to thank her collaborator and good friend, Don Mankin. She has done her best work with Don, and it is his very nature that makes that possible.

Los Angeles, California   Don Mankin
July 2004   Susan G. Cohen

The Authors

Don Mankin is founder and president of Co:e-laboration Design Associates (www.coelaboration.net), a consultancy headquartered in Los Angeles and specializing in the development of complex collaborations that involve virtual teams, diverse cultures, and multiple organizations. He earned his bachelor's degree in electrical engineering from Drexel University and his master's and doctoral degrees in engineering psychology from The Johns Hopkins University.

Mankin has more than thirty years of experience as an academic and as a consultant, speaker, and writer on issues related to virtual, international, and interorganizational collaboration; team effectiveness; technology management; innovation and human resources; and the implementation of information technology.

The author of *Toward a Post-Industrial Psychology: Emerging Perspectives on Technology, Work, Education, and Leisure* (Wiley, 1978) and first author of *Teams and Technology: Fulfilling the Promise of the New Organization* (Harvard Business School Press, 1996), he has published widely in the areas of organizational psychology and behavior. He is also lead editor of *Classics in Industrial and Organizational Psychology* (Moore, 1980).

Susan G. Cohen is a senior research scientist at the Center for Effective Organizations, Marshall School of Business, University of Southern California. She earned her bachelor's degree in psychology from the State University of New York at Buffalo, her master's degree in applied behavioral science from Whitworth College, and her doctoral degree in organizational behavior from Yale University.

Cohen has consulted and done research on a variety of approaches to improving organizational effectiveness, including group empowerment and effectiveness, employee involvement, organization development and change, participative management, performance management, and implementation of information technology. She has also done extensive research on virtual teams, self-managing work teams, and team effectiveness, particularly in settings that involve knowledge work.

She has published numerous articles and book chapters about teams and teamwork, employee involvement and empowerment, and human resource strategies, and she is coauthor of *Designing Team-Based Organizations: New Forms for Knowledge Work* (Jossey-Bass, 1995) and *Virtual Teams That Work: Creating Conditions for Virtual Team Effectiveness* (Jossey-Bass, 2003). She is also coauthor of *Teams and Technology: Fulfilling the Promise of the New Organization* (Harvard Business School Press, 1996).

Chapter One

Introduction

Business Without Boundaries
in the New Global Economy

People have worked together from the beginnings of civilization, and the forms of collaboration have barely changed since that time. Although a group of laborers building the pyramids of Egypt may seem to bear little resemblance to a team of machine operators working in a plant, the two groups actually have much in common. Both are made up of people of similar backgrounds, with clear loyalties and interests, interacting face to face to perform relatively well defined tasks in pursuit of a shared goal.

But things have changed in recent years. New technologies have made the world a smaller place and altered the nature of work. Competition and markets have become global, and knowledge is now the most important resource for organizations trying to make their way through an increasingly complex world. As a result, traditional forms of collaboration are no longer sufficient for competing effectively in this new, more demanding global business environment.

To meet constantly changing conditions and demands, business has to transcend boundaries to get what it needs regardless of where it exists—geographically, organizationally, and functionally. According to James Flanigan (2004, p. C-5), business columnist for the *Los Angeles Times*, "Companies large and small see the entire planet as a place to do business. As long as they have enough expertise, every human being on every continent is a potential employee. Borders are virtually irrelevant." In other words, we live in an era of business without boundaries, where competing effectively means collaborating across time, distance, organization, and culture. Organizations now have to go farther to find the right pieces and rapidly pull them together to create the best fit for their purposes. When circumstances change, they also have to be able to take these collaborations apart just as rapidly and start over with different pieces. In short, organizations need more complex collaborations to address the challenges of a more complex world.

These new collaborative forms are not like the teams of recent years. They may be strategic partnerships among multiple organizations with similar stakes in the outcome of the project, or they may involve virtual collaborations among people and teams working in different parts of the world. Collaborative value chains—collaborations among different organizations to produce a product or service that is primarily identified with one organization—are yet another emerging collaborative form. These collaborations are as complex as they are because of the number of people involved, the multiple organizational contexts within which they must function, and the potential psychological, cultural, and geographical distances that must be overcome. That is what this book is about: how to span these distances and transcend these boundaries to create collaborations that can address the business challenges of the new global economy.

In the next several chapters we will explore what these new, more complex collaborations look like, the challenges they face, and how to make them work. From our in-depth analysis of three case studies we will construct an action framework to help managers and executives compete successfully in the new world of global opportunities, boundary-spanning technology, and "anytime, anyplace" collaboration.

The New World of Complex Collaboration

To compete effectively in the new global economy, organizations are becoming increasingly dependent on more complex forms of collaboration. What are the characteristics of these collaborations, and what are the unique challenges they present? This is one of those situations where it's easier to define an expression by first describing its opposite—a "simple collaboration"—and then comparing a complex collaboration against this baseline. A simple collaboration is an ideal case: a situation that involves no barriers to be overcome, and where the collaborative process can flow unobstructed. The characteristics of simple collaborations and of their more complex counterparts are summarized in Table 1.1.

One characteristic of a simple collaboration is a simple task, where the inputs are predictable and manageable, and where the procedures for processing these inputs—that is, "the work"—are well defined. These are routine tasks and are characterized by low "uncertainty." In other words, both the nature and the timing of the inputs are predictable, and the procedures for dealing with these inputs are well defined and fixed. An assembly line task is an example of a task with low uncertainty: known objects (such as automobile chassis) moving down the assembly line at a predictable rate. The procedures for working on these objects—for example, mounting a particular part on each chassis—are also known, straightforward, and unvarying (see Pava, 1983).

A highly uncertain task—one in which the nature and the timing of the inputs are difficult to predict and the task procedures are

Table 1.1. Simple Versus Complex Collaborations

Simple	Complex
Well-defined task (predictable inputs, well-defined procedures, low uncertainty)	High task uncertainty
Two people	Multiple people
Few differences	High diversity (of language, goals, organizations, and so on)
Common goals	Different goals and agendas
Face-to-face contact	Virtual communication

not predetermined but require judgment—is more complex. What is typically referred to these days as "knowledge work" is characterized by high task uncertainty (Mohrman, Cohen, and Mohrman, 1995). New-product development, new-program development, process improvement, and the buying, selling, and manufacturing decisions involved in global supply chains would be examples of highly uncertain tasks.

The simplest kind of collaboration also involves only two people. With only one person, there is no collaboration, and with the addition of more than one other person the possibility of different goals, points of view, personalities, and so forth, increases significantly, as does the level of complexity.

In fact, differences of any kind make the collaborative task more complex. Two very similar people do not need to spend a great deal of time trying to understand each other's point of view, language, and expectations. The more diversity involved in the collaboration, however, the more obstacles to be overcome. By now everyone is familiar with the challenges of cultural diversity, but the challenges of organizational diversity, although less obvious, are just as important. People from different organizations who are involved in an interorganizational collaboration bring different agendas, goals, points of view, and even different cultures to the collaboration, and so these collaborations are far more challenging than they would be if the people involved were all from the same organization. Similarly, people from different functional units—engineering, manufacturing, marketing—within the same organization bring their different professional "thought worlds" (Dougherty, 1992) or cultures into the collaborative mix, and this kind of collaboration, too, is more complex than one among two like-minded engineers, for example.

Face-to-face collaboration is simpler than virtual collaboration. The immediacy, social cues, richness, and almost instantaneous reciprocity of a face-to-face interaction generally make it easier for two or more people to collaborate. But their task becomes more difficult if they have to interact via media that are less rich and more impersonal and that feature time delays between the back-and-forth responses that characterize successful collaborations.

All these factors can contribute to the complexity of a collaboration. Therefore, the important issue is not whether a collaboration is complex but how complex it is. From this definition we can see that complex collaborations go well beyond the images that typically come to mind when we think about collaboration—for example, two people who are working together on a face-to-face basis, or the internal processes that take place within intact, well-defined work teams. Complex collaborations involve individuals and formal teams, but they also encompass much more. Different individuals, teams, organizations, and cultures, often in dispersed locations, combine in various combinations to comprise the types of collaborations that are the focus of this book. The important thing is to understand that the more complex the collaboration, the more difficult it is, and the more effort is required to make it work. The challenge is to overcome the difficulty, to compensate for the complexity.

Showing how to do this is the purpose of this book.

An Action Framework for Designing Complex Collaborations

All collaborations, complex or otherwise, have the same foundation: people, the relationships among them, and the interpersonal processes that enable the people to work together. This is where collaboration begins; it is the petri dish within which collaboration breeds, grows, and develops. The success of any collaboration depends first and foremost on the people involved in it and on the nature and quality of their interrelationships and interactions.

As the discussion in the previous section suggests, however, complexity can distract or overwhelm even the most skilled, well-intentioned, and motivated collaborators. Therefore, the challenge is to manage complexity so that it enhances and energizes the collaboration instead of destroying it. We will show in the chapters that follow that the key is structure: well-defined roles, expectations, responsibilities, decision-making processes, and the like, make it easier for participants to get a handle on the many issues, problems, and challenges they have to face in making a complex collaboration work. Structure helps to focus action, informs decisions, serves as a buffer against distraction, and improves efficiency. Structure in and of itself is not the essence of collaboration, but it does reduce uncertainty and confusion and increases predictability, and it can make complex collaborations less complex and more manageable. The more complex the collaboration, the more structure is needed. Structure creates a zone of stability within which creative collaborations can develop and thrive.

These two dimensions—people and their relationships, on the one hand (the "soft" side of complex collaboration), and structure, on the other—are, of course, related and inseparable: structure supports collaborative relationships, and collaborative relationships can produce structure. These two dimensions are like intertwined threads weaving through the cases we present in this book and through our action framework. Both threads are needed in stitching up the fabric of complex collaborations; without both, the garment falls apart. These are the fundamental truths, the DNA, that underlie our action framework and our perspective on how to make complex collaborations work.

The Action Framework

The broad outline of our action framework is presented in Figure 1.1. In many respects, our action framework is similar to other, generic models for project management and organizational change (see, for example, Mohrman and Cummings, 1989). The difference with our framework is that we pay special attention to the challenges that arise when projects require collaboration across temporal, geographical, organizational, and cultural boundaries. How to structure, facilitate, and support these kinds of collaborations is the primary focus of the framework as we present it in this book.

The framework is composed of four loosely defined, overlapping phases linked in an upward-moving spiral.

- *Phase I: Setting the Stage*. This is the phase of getting organizations ready for complex collaborations in general. In essence, this phase creates the potential and provides the impetus for moving forward.
- *Phase II: Getting Started with Specific Projects*. This is the phase of initiating specific projects through the efforts of key people working together. Creating collaborative relationships among key people is one of the most critical steps in this phase.

Figure 1.1. The Four Phases of the Action Framework

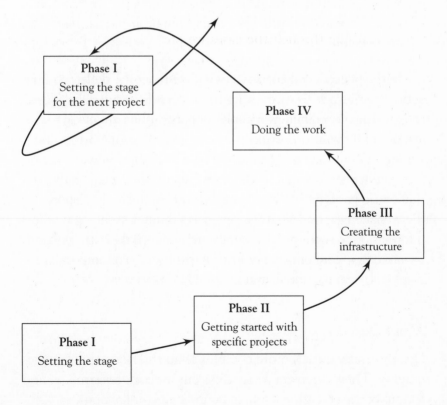

- *Phase III: Creating the Infrastructure.* This is the phase of developing the structure for the project, especially those elements that support collaboration, and outlining the processes to be followed in carrying out the project.

- *Phase IV: Doing the Work.* This is the phase of carrying out project tasks, and of revisiting and revising the infrastructure and the processes as needed. While participants are doing the work, they can also learn from their successes and failures and use that information to modify their goals, plans, and tasks. Ultimately, these learnings can be used to develop the collaborative capabilities of the organization in general, setting the stage for even more ambitious collaborations down the road. That is why we depict two Phase I's in Figure 1.1. Each project does not end where it begins but instead sets the stage for a new round of complex collaborations built on experience and knowledge gained from projects that have come before.

In the next several chapters we will flesh out the skeleton of our action framework by examining three very different cases. These cases feature very different complex collaborations involving a variety of organizations pursuing diverse goals and operating under varying circumstances. The cases enable us to show how the action framework plays out in real life as we recount the actual challenges that participants faced, what they did and did not do in response to these challenges, and what happened as a result. On the basis of this information we will identify specific action steps that other organizations can follow in collaborating across their own temporal, geographical, organizational, and cultural boundaries.

About Our Cases

Our three cases, each more complex than the last, are also wide-ranging. They touch on many different aspects, enterprises, and regions of the emerging world of boundaryless collaboration:

- Training programs for construction equipment service technicians
- Development of electronic games
- Manufacture of sophisticated computer network technology
- Construction equipment dealerships in the heartland of North America
- Product engineering teams in Hong Kong
- Factories in southern China
- High-tech companies in Silicon Valley

We chose to examine a small number of cases in depth instead of concentrating on a larger number of less intensive cases narrowly focused on specific practices, and our choice was dictated by the nature of our subject. Complex phenomena require complex cases to illustrate the many interrelated elements that make up those phenomena. In the next several chapters, we will show that the whole of a complex collaboration is greater than the sum of its parts—that, for example, the personal qualities of the collaborators mean little unless the collaborators have the opportunity to form relationships, and that these relationships are supported by communication systems and well-defined roles and procedures. It would have been difficult to show the interactions among critical success factors if our cases had not been rich enough to illustrate the interdependence among those factors. An in-depth case can also reveal the dynamic interplay among people, processes, and events as a collaboration develops, and as the success factors play out over time. Not only can in-depth examination demonstrate the final result, it can also show how successful outcomes were reached. A case studied in depth over time provides a moving picture, not just a snapshot.

For the most part, our cases feature successful projects. Examining these projects closely, we could begin to identify what made these collaborations work, and, by extension, what might make similar collaborations successful. But even in these successful cases, things did not always go well. Sometimes decisions were not executed effectively, and the participants occasionally overlooked critical issues and failed to do what needed to be done. We learned from these failures of omission and commission as well as from what actually did work.

The first case features *interorganizational collaborations* among the John Deere Construction & Forestry Equipment Company and various John Deere dealerships and two-year technical colleges throughout the United States. The purpose of the collaborations was to develop training programs for technicians who serviced John Deere construction equipment; these service technicians were in short supply at the time the program was initiated. The case describes the overall program run by Deere—which initiates, facilitates, and supports these programs nationwide—as well as two projects, one in Minnesota and the other in Texas, that were conducted under the auspices of the new program.

This was the first case we examined, and we had the opportunity to follow it over an extended period. As a result, we were able to observe the ebb and flow of a long-term project, from the initial uncertainties as participants from different organizations felt each other out through the development of critical relationships and trust to the eventual pulling back as changing economic conditions led to different priorities. Therefore, when we talk about transcending the boundaries of time in complex collaborations, we are also talking about duration, not just time zones.

The second case shifts the focus to *cross-cultural collaboration*, particularly collaboration across international boundaries. Only one company was involved in this case, the Radica Games Group, Inc., one of the world's leading developers and manufacturers of hand-held electronic games and video game controllers. This case also included two major projects, the development of the Bass Fishin' game in the mid-1990s and a more recent set of projects to develop controllers for the video game consoles produced by Nintendo, Sony, and Microsoft. The Bass Fishin' game project involved different teams in Dallas, Hong Kong, and Radica's factory in southern China; the controller projects involved the same sites in addition to a team from a company in the United Kingdom that was acquired by Radica in the late 1990s. The international nature of this case enabled us to take a close look at the challenges of collaboration across great distances, numerous time zones, and dramatically different cultures. The nature of the project and of the industry—product development in the toy and game business—adds another dimension to this case: the impact of intense time and performance pressures.

Like the John Deere case, our third case also features an interorganizational collaboration, but with a very important difference. In a *supply-chain collaboration*, interorganizational collaboration is more than just the means to an end. Companies like Solectron, the primary organization in our third case, have evolved in recent years from contract manufacturers to global supply-chain facilitators. Their role now involves facilitating the entire supply chain, not just acting as one of the links in the chain. As a result, complex interorganizational collaborations are now the very core of such companies' business and their most important product.

Solectron is one of the pioneers in the electronics manufacturing services industry, an industry that is emblematic of the increasingly global and interorganizational nature of modern manufacturing. Because close collaboration is intrinsic to supply chains, the collaborations in the Solectron case were more tightly linked and critical to the success of all the parties involved than they were in the John Deere case. In fact, close collaboration with customers and suppliers is a particularly important element in Solectron's new strategic direction. This case shows how Solectron executes this strategy and supports the company's new emphasis on the close relationships that are so crucial to Solectron's future. We also examine one of the company's most far-reaching efforts to date, Solectron's close collaboration with one of its customers, Brocade, a producer of data network storage systems.

Comments

For each case, we interviewed between twenty and twenty-five people, mostly in face-to-face meetings, who either were directly involved in the collaborations or were close enough to the projects to provide additional details and supplementary perspectives. Except in the John Deere case, the actual names of all the interviewees are used, as are the names of the organizations they represent. The names of the John Deere participants are real, but the names of organizations and individuals outside John Deere are fictitious.

For the most part, our cases cover a limited period of time, and each one is reasonably accurate for that time period. But things change, people leave, and new information comes out. We did try to update our information as much as possible, but at some point we had to put an end to gathering information and making interpretations and bring each case to a conclusion. In addition, our three cases as a group represent a wide range of organization types, products, services, outcomes, and collaborative forms. They clearly do not represent all possibilities, but they are sufficiently diverse to give us a degree of confidence in the general applicability of the recommendations that emerge from our analyses. It is our firm belief that more follow-up and additional cases would have added little to our conclusions and recommendations.

Plan of the Book

The three cases are presented in Chapters Two through Six. The description and analysis of the John Deere case are presented entirely in Chapter Two. To each of the other two cases we devote two chapters, a choice that reflects their greater complexity. Specifically, Chapter Three describes the Radica case, and Chapter Four analyzes the case in terms of our action framework, whereas Chapters Five and Six follow the same pattern for the Solectron case.

Because the individual case analyses provide only pieces of the puzzle, Chapters Seven and Eight pull all the pieces together—that is, all the action steps suggested by each case—into our comprehensive action framework for collaborating across time, distance, organization, and culture. At the end of Chapter Eight we conclude the book by returning to our two "threads"—structure and collaborative relationships—and exploring how they might be applied, as a speculative rule of thumb, to all complex collaborations: those that are current, and those that may evolve and emerge in the years to come.

Chapter Two

Across Organizations

The John Deere Construction & Forestry Technology Program

Despite the focus of the last few years on new technology, globalization, and the rapidly changing world of business, not all complex collaborations are manifestations of the so-called new economy. It is perhaps fitting, then, that we begin with a case that is decidedly "old economy" in its focus and look. But, as we will show by the end of this book, many of the principles illustrated by this case are universal and enduring.

The case focuses on collaborations between Deere & Company (the manufacturer of John Deere agricultural, construction, and forestry equipment) and several John Deere equipment dealerships and two-year community/technical colleges throughout North America. The purpose of the collaborations was to develop and offer college-based programs to train technicians who can service John Deere equipment.

Deere & Company is one of the oldest industrial companies in the United States. From its modest beginnings in 1837 as a one-man blacksmith shop, it has grown into a *Fortune* 100 company, with total sales and revenues of almost $15.5 billion in fiscal year 2003. Deere is the world's leading manufacturer of agricultural equipment and a leader in the production of construction and forestry equipment.

The company sells almost all its equipment through a worldwide network of dealerships. Most of the dealerships are independently owned, although Deere & Company does hold a significant ownership interest in some. The dealerships are typically made up of different dealer "stores" in different locations. The agreement between Deere and its dealerships gives them the right to sell and service John Deere equipment within particular regions or areas. In return, the dealerships agree not to sell any products in those areas that compete with John Deere products. The manufacturer-dealer relationship is at the heart of the industry and played a critical role in the projects that comprise this case.

"New Economy" Challenges for an "Old Economy" Company

Despite Deere's origins in the agricultural era and its Industrial Age history and image, Deere is very much a postindustrial company with a global presence. It does business in more than 160 countries and employs approximately forty-three thousand people worldwide. As business journalist James Flanigan notes (2003, p. C-1), Deere and its closest competitors, Caterpillar and Cummins, "are examples of how U.S. industry has fundamentally changed in the last decade. All three of these major corporations . . . now operate seamlessly on all continents with design, production, supply and marketing staffs working in Asia for Asia, Europe for Europe and North America for the United States, Canada and Mexico."

Just as Deere's manufacturing processes have evolved, so have its products. Like so many other products that have come to define the postindustrial era, John Deere equipment has become more knowledge-based. Construction machines now rely heavily on electronics and other advanced technologies, presenting new challenges to the technicians responsible for servicing this machinery. In the words of Richard Park, manager of the John Deere program that is the focus of this case, "Our equipment is changing today; it is much more complex than it was in the past. Now more than ever, it's critically important—to the dealers, to the customers and to us—that the people working on those machines are well qualified. It's not something they could have learned through twenty years of experience being a mechanic. There is new technology, new tools, new skills. It is in our interest to have technicians working on these machines who know what they are doing."

Deere, its dealers, and its customers not only need technicians who are better trained and more highly skilled, they also need more of them. In the late 1990s, when the training program was started, service technicians for construction equipment were in short supply, and the shortage was rapidly getting worse. The shortage was the result of two complementary sets of circumstances: an expanding economy throughout most of the decade, and an apparent preference among young people at that time for "sexier" careers that had more status and appeal (for example, in computers and Internet applications).

This shortage had significant financial implications both for the manufacturers of this equipment and for the dealers who sold it. John Deere customers, typically construction companies, expect reliable service for the lifetime of the equipment. In the words of one John Deere dealer, "They [the customers] will trade their souls for uptime." As a result, the basis for competition in this market is increasingly product support. Therefore, Deere can sell more equipment if its customers can count on skilled technicians to keep the equipment up and running. For the dealers, the benefits are even greater and more immediate. "After-market" service is now one of the fastest-growing sources of revenue for dealers, frequently surpassing the profits derived from the sale of the equipment itself. In fact, profit margins for service are as much as five times greater than for sales. Given the potential implications for manufacturers, dealers, and customers, it is easy to see why, at the time this training program was initiated, a leading publication in the construction equipment industry concluded "the urgency to supply equipment service departments with qualified technicians affects and even overshadows just about every other industry concern at the turn of the century" (McGinty, 1999, p. 25).

About the Case: The Construction & Forestry Technology Program

Because of these concerns, managers from several leading John Deere construction equipment dealerships met in late 1998 with the management of Deere's Construction Equipment Division to push for the development of a program to train new service technicians. Two earlier attempts to develop similar programs had met with limited success, so Deere and the representatives from the dealerships made a commitment to learn from the limitations of the earlier programs and develop a new program that would better meet the needs of the dealers and their customers. Mick Sims, a Deere product support manager at the time, was assigned to spearhead the new effort.

Mick found a promising model for the new program in the similar but more successful "Ag Tech" Program offered by Deere's Agricultural Equipment Division. He worked with the dealer representatives and Deere management to adapt the Ag Tech model to fit the new program's needs, and the Construction Equipment Technology Program was ready to go by early 1999. Mick quickly found the first site for the new program, at Southwest Georgia Technical College, and the program was soon under way. The name of both the division and the program was changed two years later, when the division purchased Timberjack, Inc., to form the new John Deere Construction & Forestry Company, a division of the parent organization, Deere & Co.

The Construction & Forestry Technology (C&F Tech) Program is designed to help develop training programs for service technicians in various regions of the country where needs are particularly acute. By the summer of 2003 there were seven C&F Tech two-year associate degree programs at seven different colleges throughout the United States. Each program involves a collaboration among three types of organizations: a manufacturer of construction equipment (the John Deere Construction & Forestry Company), regionally based dealerships that sell this equipment, and a two-year community/technical college in the same region as the dealers. All three partners play crucial but different roles in the development and implementation of the programs.

The John Deere Construction & Forestry Company supplies components and tools for students to use in their training. It sponsors annual meetings at Deere headquarters in Moline, Illinois, for students and instructors across all the programs, and it provides other resources and support to the individual programs. Possibly the most important contribution made by Deere is the people who help get the programs going and keep them running with their support, effort, and time. They include the director of the overall program and the field staff who sit on the advisory committee for each program.

Despite the corporation's highly visible role in facilitating and supporting the programs, the dealers and the colleges are the ones responsible for the day-to-day details. Mick Sims designed the programs to be dealer-driven because the dealers are the ones who have the most to gain from the program—that is, a future supply of well-trained technicians who will make money for the dealerships by servicing the equipment they sell. Therefore, the dealers are expected to make the greatest investment. Most of that investment involves finding, recruiting, and supporting the students via tuition stipends and summer internships, and then hiring them when they graduate. The dealers also provide equipment for the hands-on component of the students' training. The colleges, of course, are also critical to the success of this collaboration. They provide instruction, instructional material, and the use of their facilities in addition to the same services and support that they provide to their other students. All three parties—Deere, the dealerships, and the colleges—collaborate on the development of the curriculum.

Let us now take a closer look at the two programs that comprise this case.

The Central Minnesota College Program

The Central Minnesota College (CMC) Program grew out of an earlier project involving ABC Equipment Company and a two-year technical college (not CMC) near ABC headquarters, in a city in the northern tier of the central United States. The focus of the earlier program had been on retraining experienced technicians rather than on training new ones. Support from ABC's dealer network was lukewarm because of the dealers' concern about losing the services of their technicians, as well as the revenues associated with those services, while their technicians were undergoing retraining. For this reason, and given the press of other issues with higher priority, this program was unable to attract a high-level champion at ABC who could provide active, hands-on leadership and support.

After the demise of this program, in early 1998, Don Garnet, the coordinator of the program for ABC, left the company and took a position as an instructor at CMC. Shortly thereafter, Don and Myra Holt, ABC's director of training, began discussing the possibility of trying again, this time with CMC as their partner. Before long they heard about the Deere Construction Technology Program. Mick Sims had already launched the first program in Georgia and was aggressively looking for new sites. ABC and CMC decided to join forces with Deere by redirecting the focus of their program from retraining experienced technicians to training new ones. By July 1999 the Deere/ABC/Central Minnesota College collaboration was under way.

This change in the program's focus, coupled with the involvement and support of Deere, made it easier to find an executive champion at ABC and to gain the support of ABC's dealer network—the missing links from the program that had failed only a couple of years earlier. ABC soon hired Joan Jackson to take over the day-to-day tasks of managing this collaboration from the ABC side. Her counterpart on the CMC side was Beverly Carter, who had twenty years of experience at CMC in developing customized training programs for local businesses. Mick Sims, of course, represented Deere. Mick wanted to get more dealers involved in recruiting students for the program, and so he invited another John Deere distributor, Northland Equipment Company, to join the collaboration in October 1999. In January 2000, a proposal was submitted to the Minnesota Job Skills Partnership to help fund the development and implementation of the program. The award of the grant, in the spring, marked the official beginning of the project.

Things did not go smoothly at first. The representative from Northland left the company shortly after he was assigned to the project. When Northland did not immediately replace him, the other partners feared that Northland was not fully committed to the project. In addition, a number of ABC employees left that company for jobs at Northland shortly after the project began, taking advantage of opportunities created by the greater contact between the two dealerships through the project. Joan Jackson and others at ABC worried that these job moves foreshadowed an unexpected and undesirable project outcome: future competition between ABC and Northland for the service technicians who would eventually graduate from the program.

Joan, looking back on this time and these events, noted in one of our interviews that the underlying problem was that she didn't "know the company [Northland] and had no person to contact . . . no relationship with a representative from Northland to help resolve the issues." As a result, "all of the little issues were magnified." The bottom line was that all these changes, coupled with Joan's lack of a relationship with a trusted and familiar contact person at Northland, created a cloud of uncertainty about Northland's commitment to the project and about the company's intentions regarding the students who were being sponsored by ABC's dealer stores.

What ultimately resolved the crisis was Northland's appointment of Derek Smith, the company's manager of human resources, to represent the company on the project team. His appointment eliminated the other team members' concerns about Northland's commitment to the project. Perhaps most important, Derek's appointment gave Joan someone to work with in resolving lingering concerns about potential competition between ABC and Northland. It did not take Derek and Joan long to form a close working relationship and reach a "gentleman's agreement" not to actively recruit each other's program graduates.

The project proceeded relatively smoothly from that point on. The team members worked well together and were able to develop strong, amicable relationships. They did encounter other difficulties, of course, but nothing that threatened the project as much as the initial misunderstandings, or at least nothing directly related to their interpersonal processes or to the design of the collaboration itself. Aside from those just described, their greatest difficulties had to do with the passage of time and with the inevitable impact that changing conditions and priorities have on long-term projects and programs. Before we turn to these issues, let us take a brief look at the other program in this case, and at the very different challenges that the participants had to overcome in achieving the successes that they did, as limited as those successes were.

The Prairie College Program

The purpose of the project at Prairie College was essentially the same as that of the CMC project: to develop a two-year associate degree program for construction and forestry equipment service technicians. The major difference was the region to be served by the program—in this project, central Texas instead of Minnesota. Therefore, some of the players were also different. Deere and Company was involved, of course, as was ABC, since that company had a number of dealers in the region. Several other dealerships with a presence in the region were also involved.

The origins of the program at Prairie College were different from those of the CMC program. Prairie College was already offering several successful programs in partnership with Deere & Company when Dave Harsha, a Deere representative from Dallas, visited the campus, along with a manager from an ABC store in the area, to discuss the possibility of developing a C&F Tech Program there. Prairie College decided to go ahead with the new program and put it under the direction of the same faculty member who managed the other Deere programs on campus. This faculty member was appropriately nicknamed "Dr. Deere," a name reflecting not only his Ph.D. in English literature but also his many years of experience as a diesel mechanic. Because of Deere and Company's insistence that the C&F Tech Programs be widely supported by dealers throughout their regions, several other dealerships in the area soon joined Deere, ABC, and Prairie College in this collaboration.

Like the project at CMC, the one at Prairie College hit some bumps in the road. Unlike the CMC project, the Prairie College project also hit an axle-crunching pothole. The bumps slowed the project down at critical times, but the pothole eventually brought the program to a grinding halt.

The first bump appeared at the beginning of the project, with the confusion created by the sheer number of different dealerships and dealer stores that were involved. The confusion was especially acute for the participants from Prairie College, who only had to work with Deere in the development of the college's earlier programs but now had to deal with what was, from their perspective, a bewildering number of different organizations. The Prairie College participants initially had considerable difficulty sorting out all the other participants and stakeholders. In comparison with the development of the earlier programs at Prairie College, the structure of this one was more complex, the number of parties to be dealt with was much larger, and influences and authority were more diffuse. Not surprisingly, "Dr. Deere" was often confused about whom to contact for equipment, tools, and parts. To resolve this issue, Dave Harsha was designated as the single point of contact for "Dr. Deere" where the program's equipment needs were concerned. In the project's early months, frequent face-to-face meetings also helped everyone sort out the players as well as their roles and responsibilities and the expertise they brought to the project.

Instructor turnover was what finally killed the program at Prairie College. For a variety of reasons, the program went through three instructors in less than two years, and it never fully recovered. Six of the twelve students in the first class dropped out before the end of the first year. Problems with student enrollment and attrition continued for the next two years. In the spring of 2003 Prairie College, facing severe budget cuts from the state legislature and the continued prospect of disappointing enrollments, decided to drop the program. The program was quickly picked up, however, by Texas State Technical College (the institution's actual name), in Waco, and the Prairie College students have since been transferred to this new "home," with minimal disruption.

Current State and Future Plans

As the fate of the program at Prairie College suggests, the overall results of the C&F Tech Program have been mixed. By the summer of 2003 the seven existing C&F Tech Programs had graduated about 60 students, and 120 were enrolled. These numbers were significantly lower than expected. The original plan had called for as many as fifteen programs by 2003, but the number of programs was down from the peak of nine, a milestone that had been reached two years earlier. The original plan had also called for 18 students per year in each program, whereas actual enrollments were less than half that total.

One reason for these disappointing results was the sluggish economy that followed the "new economy" boom of the 1990s. Many of the dealers, faced with flat sales and revenues, were reluctant to commit time and resources to a distant and uncertain pay-off. Their attention was elsewhere—on staying profitable rather than on developing technicians who would not be available for full-time work for at least two years. There was still a shortage of technicians, but it felt less urgent at the time, in the context of the economic conditions. The difficult economy and these somewhat disappointing results also had an impact on the motivation and commitment of some of the participants, and so it should come as no surprise that interactions among them became less easygoing than they had once been.

The good news is that the quality of the students and the graduates has been anything but disappointing. The consensus among all participants, including the instructors who teach them and the dealers that hire them, is that the students are very well trained. Richard Park, the current director of the program at Deere and Company, consistently hears glowing reports about the C&F Tech Program graduates. According to Park, they apparently are climbing their career ladders faster than their peers and are taking on more responsibility and reaching higher levels sooner than expected.

In view of these mixed results, the original goals for the C&F Tech Program have been modified to fit more realistically into the limitations imposed by the economy and by the nature of the program itself. Deere still views the program as important but not critical to the company's long-term success. Further development is not a high priority, and so Deere has no plans to expand the program beyond the seven schools that currently participate. As a result, the emphasis has shifted from growth to consolidation—for example, updating the program, improving student recruiting, and developing new and more cost-efficient curriculum models. Because Park's role is now primarily advisory, and because there are no plans to expand the program to new schools, he devotes only about 10 percent of his time to the program, as compared with the approximately 80 percent that Mick Sims spent in the early years.

In summary, the story of the C&F Tech Program is complicated. The participants faced and overcame numerous challenges and achieved a number of successes over the course of several years, and yet they were not able to make these successes stick. They did achieve their primary objective—the development of training programs for service technicians—but they were not able to attract enough students to sustain the programs in their initial forms and locations.

Why was this so? Was it just the economy? Was it something the participants did or failed to do? Or did the nature of the project place insurmountable obstacles in the path of unrealistic goals? In the rest of this chapter we will examine these projects more closely, to see what we can learn from what the participants did (or did not do) and to identify the actions that others might take in designing and implementing their own complex collaborations.

Phase I: Setting the Stage

Deere took a number of steps to set the stage for the interorganizational collaborations described in this case. These steps fall into two distinct categories. One category is general and broadly defined, dealing as it does with issues of culture. The other category could not be more different, because it involves the development and implementation of a specific program for initiating and supporting interorganizational collaborations. Despite these differences, the categories and the action steps within them are intrinsically related, with the second category complementing and reflecting the culture described in the first. The action steps in both categories, as well as those associated with the later phases of our action framework, are summarized in Table 2.1.

Promote a Culture of Extraorganizational Relationships

All the organizations involved in these projects had previous experience with interorganizational collaboration. Deere's C&F Tech Program had already initiated projects at other schools before embarking on the collaborations described in this chapter. Other Deere divisions, particularly the Agricultural Equipment Division, had long histories with similar programs. Both colleges had also collaborated with other companies and industries to develop external technical training programs. Moreover, the dealerships' business, by its very nature, is built on their relationship with the manufacturer of the equipment they sell. All of this previous experience seemed to have created, in the words of one of the administrators at CMC, "a culture of [interorganizational] relationships."

How can an organization and its leaders create a culture of interorganizational relationships? Relationships between these manufacturers and their dealers have been the cornerstone of the industry since its earliest days, and so it is apparent that senior management views these relationships as an important element in their organizations' long-term strategy. They frequently talk about these relationships and engage in activities that reinforce the culture. One of the best examples of this explicit and intentional link between strategy, culture, and action can be seen in the John Deere program that is the focus of this case.

Support Collaboration Through Programs and Other Explicit Activities

Deere's Construction and Forestry Technology Program is a product of this culture and an excellent example of how to reinforce and promote it. This program is the "umbrella" for Deere's complex collaborations with John Deere dealerships and community/technical colleges throughout the country. Just as important as the program itself is what the company did to make it work. Besides the equipment, annual meetings, and symbolic "capital" associated with the Deere name, the most important thing the company did was to give Mick Sims the time and resources he needed to do his job.

Apparently Deere also chose the right person for the job. Mick was outgoing, personable, and passionate about the program. He was also comfortable interacting with people from different organizations, with different backgrounds, and in different career tracks and jobs, including technicians, managers, and academics. This last quality, which encompasses what we refer to as "lateral skills," is particularly important in the kind of boundary-crossing collaboration that we talk about throughout this book. All the key people in our cases display this quality to some degree. Because lateral skills play an especially critical role in getting specific projects started and keeping them going, we will have much more to say about these skills.

Table 2.1. Action Steps from the John Deere Case

Phase	Action Step
Phase I: Setting the Stage	*Promote a culture of extraorganizational relationships* Make it a strategic priority Be public about it *Support collaboration through programs and other explicit activities* Set up programs Appoint people who have lateral skills Give the appointed people the needed time and resources
Phase II: Getting Started with Specific Projects	*Find appropriate partners* with shared goals, complementary capabilities, and compatible cultures *Gain top management's support* If project is not top-down, get high-level support (executive champion) ASAP *Get access to critical resources,* from other sources if necessary *Put the right people in the right place* Create liaison roles Fill liaison roles with people who have good lateral skills *Link the liaisons in collaborative pairs* Use face-to-face interaction to build relationships within pairs Create pairs at management level(s) as well, to provide oversight, escalation paths for resolving conflicts, and so on

Phase III:
Creating the Infrastructure

Create a structure for governance and authority
Create an advisory committee and an implementation team
Use an adaptable, shared, facilitative approach to leadership (more directive and driving early on)

Formalize roles, relationships, and understandings
Formally identify and define roles
Make sure roles and structure are as simple and clear as possible
Develop a contract or a charter to codify the governance/authority structure, roles, relationships, understandings, and so on

Meet and communicate frequently, and keep external stakeholders informed

Learn from doing and adapt
Regularly share ideas and experiences
Monitor progress and conditions
As necessary, modify goals and plans

Phase IV:
Doing the Work

Phase II: Getting Started with Specific Projects

With the overall program in place, the right person (Mick Sims) running the program, and the resources allocated to support Mick's efforts, the stage was set for moving forward. This case suggests that four kinds of activities are required to get particular projects started. First, one or more people have to initiate the project by finding appropriate partners. Second, unless these initiators are high-level managers, they have to gain explicit support for the project from top management. Third, the right people must be put in the right place to carry the program out. Fourth, these people should then be linked in collaborative relationships.

Find Appropriate Partners

Mick's first task was to find partners with similar goals. All the organizations involved in the program shared the same goal: to develop programs for expanding the pool of well-trained service technicians. This shared goal is why the dealers and Deere were willing to provide equipment that they otherwise could have sold to generate immediate profits. This is also why the colleges were willing to provide facilities that they could have used for other purposes. And it is why all the organizations were willing to assign key people to work on the project. Of course, the reasons why each organization was committed to this goal differed—for example, the colleges wanted to increase student enrollment, Deere wanted to make money by selling equipment, and the dealers wanted to make money by both selling and servicing the equipment. But they all recognized that they could achieve their individual goals by working together to achieve their shared goals.

Mick also needed partners with different but complementary capabilities. Each partner in the C&F Tech collaborations offered knowledge, skills, resources, and capabilities that could not be provided by the others, or at least not as well. The colleges offered expertise in curriculum development and instruction, Deere offered equipment and experience from other projects, and the dealers offered service expertise, scholarships, and internships. Overall, these complementary capabilities created a synergy among the separate organizations that was far greater than the sum of its parts.

Mick also had to make sure that the cultures of the collaborating organizations were compatible. The cultural compatibility among the dealers, and between the dealers and Deere, is obvious. All the dealers in each project are in the same line of business, distribute the same equipment from the same manufacturer, and are in the same general region. Their values and objectives are similar, they speak pretty much the same language, and most have comparable backgrounds. Deere's culture is in many respects similar to that of the dealers: people at Deere are all involved in the construction equipment industry, if in different aspects of it, and so they share many of the same values and concerns.

Between the dealerships and Deere, on the one hand, and the colleges, on the other, we also see similarities in culture, or, at the very least, significant compatibilities. Two-year community/technical colleges, even though they are academic institutions, have much in common with construction equipment manufacturers and dealerships. Their mission is to serve the needs of employers like Deere, ABC, and Northland. Furthermore, many of their instructors, like Don Garnet at CMC, who previously worked at ABC, have worked for the very companies that will hire the students they train. Therefore, community/technical colleges are inextricably linked to this world and share many of its values and norms.

It is also important to note that Mick was not the only person in this case searching for partners with shared goals, complementary capabilities, and compatible cultures. Don at CMC and Myra Holt at ABC were each engaged in a similar search for compatible partners as they explored the possibility of a collaboration to resurrect the program that had failed a few years earlier at another school. Their decision to develop their program under the John

Deere C&F Tech umbrella reflects the same process, as did their decision to refocus the program—from the retraining of experienced technicians to the training of new ones—and bring their goals into line with those of the Deere program.

Gain Top Management's Support

The start-up of the C&F Tech Program at CMC illustrates that projects do not always get started or driven from the top down. Sometimes a project emerges from prior relationships and chance interactions among people at various levels of an organization. Neither Myra nor Don was a senior executive, nor were their interactions driven by an explicit mandate from their respective executives. The origins of the CMC program were more bottom-up or middle-out than top-down. The Prairie College project, by contrast, was initiated pretty much from the top down, at least from the standpoint of the college. These differences in the origins of the two programs indicate that complex collaborations can get started in many ways: from the top down, from the middle out, from the bottom up, or in a combination of some or all of these ways.

Comparing the origins of the CMC program with those of its predecessor suggests an important action step for projects that start from the bottom up or the middle out. Like the CMC program, the earlier program was started from the bottom up by an employee at ABC in collaboration with a local technical college. Unlike the CMC program, the earlier program was not able to attract high-level management support at ABC, so it didn't last long. The later program, also a bottom-up/middle-out effort, was much more successful in attracting a high-level project champion at ABC, and therefore it went much farther. The lesson from this example is very clear: when projects are not initially driven from the top down but emerge instead from bottom-up/middle-out collaborations, high-level management support is needed to move the project forward. The sooner this support is found, the sooner the project can get started.

This case illustrates as well that high-level support is also important for keeping projects going. When there was high-level support from all the partners, the projects moved along, and when there wasn't, the projects stalled. It is no coincidence that the point at which the CMC project experienced the most trouble was the brief period of uncertainty about management's support at Northland, when the company was slow to replace its original representative after his departure from the company. The other side of that coin is how well the project progressed after that, when Northland's management assigned Derek Smith to the project and provided him with the time and resources he needed to work closely with the other representatives. Another, even more dramatic example of the impact of high-level support—or, in this case, the lack thereof—came at the end of the Prairie College project, when the school's executive leadership decided to drop the program.

Get Access to Critical Resources

Providing access to such critical resources as time and money is one of the most important roles for the project's executive sponsor, but the search for resources should not stop there. The John Deere case demonstrates that the search for resources can reach even beyond the boundaries of the organizations directly involved in the collaboration. In the Central Minnesota College project, for example, the grant from the Minnesota Job Skills Partnership is what ultimately made the program possible. Similarly, a grant from the Deere Foundation provided the funds for remodeling the building that Prairie College purchased to house the new program. Without the grant, the building would have not been ready for the first class, and yet another pothole would have appeared in the already bumpy road traveled by this complex and difficult collaboration. Of course, most private sector projects would not qualify for public or foundation funding, but public-private partnerships are not uncommon these days, and so this is clearly a critical step in any interorganizational collaboration involving nonprofit or not-for-profit partners.

Put the Right People in the Right Place

Mick Sims was the right person in the right place to get the C&F Tech Program started: he brought critical skills to a critical role. If either piece of this equation had been missing, the program would never have gotten off the ground. We could say the same thing about Myra and Don, who got the CMC project started, and about Joan, Beverly Carter, and Derek, who kept it going. "Dr. Deere" and Dave Harsha played similar roles in the Prairie College project. These examples suggest a number of action steps that need to be taken in initiating and sustaining complex collaborations. Collectively, these action steps are excellent embodiments of the theme we introduced in Chapter 1: the intertwined threads of structure and relationships that are woven throughout our action framework.

In speaking of the "right place," we refer to formal roles created for the explicit purpose of linking the different organizations involved in a complex collaboration—in other words, liaison roles. Although Mick and the others never formally used this expression, it is clear that they played these essential roles in the C&F Tech projects. In most cases, liaison roles were explicitly created by each organization to represent its interests and link it to the other organizations. But it was putting the right people in these roles that literally made the roles come alive, transforming good intentions into an actual vehicle for effective participation and collaboration.

What personal qualities of the people in these roles made it possible for the projects to achieve the successes they did, in some very difficult and limiting circumstances? Almost all our interviewees, when asked to describe the factors that made their projects successful, cited the qualities of one or more of the liaison people already mentioned. The interviewees were fairly consistent in describing specific qualities; most noted that the people in liaison roles possessed a good sense of humor, were easygoing, demonstrated enthusiasm, had a positive attitude, and the like. In other words, they all seemed to possess good interpersonal skills. This is not a surprising finding, of course, but the particular qualities that our interviewees described show a more detailed picture of what the expression "the right people in the right place" actually means when we are talking about collaboration.

As we suggested earlier, one of the most important components of interpersonal competence is what we refer to as "lateral skills," which encompass the ability to "work effectively with people of different functional backgrounds, work experiences, knowledge bases and skills" (Mankin, Cohen, and Bikson, 1996, p. 97). Despite the fact that most of the participants had similar backgrounds and experiences, there were some noteworthy differences, particularly between Joan at ABC and Beverly at CMC. Their relationship was critical in keeping the project moving forward during its difficult early months. On the surface, at least, Joan and Beverly seemed to have little in common. These two women, as described by Joan, were "the cover of Ms." (Joan), on the one hand, and "the good Lutheran mom," on the other. They were able to transcend their differences, however, and find common ground so that they could work together toward their shared goals. Our interviews and observations suggest that several qualities—empathy, openness, and the ability to respect and appreciate the different competencies and perspectives that others bring to successful collaborations—may be associated with good lateral skills.

Perhaps the best way to understand the difference between merely good interpersonal skills and the more important lateral skills is to imagine a person who might best be described as a "congenial racist." This is a person who gets along well with people who are similar in background and outlook and whose roots are in the same culture. But this is also a person who has difficulty relating to anyone who is different, has different experiences or points of view, or comes from a different cultural background. It takes a person with good lateral skills to work with someone who is very different. This set of skills is far more valuable than garden-variety good interpersonal skills—particularly in today's multicultural, cross-functional, interorganizational workplace, and it is a skill set that is much more difficult to find.

Link the Liaisons in Collaborative Pairs

The example of Joan and Beverly suggests another important step in getting complex collaborations started. In both projects discussed in this case we found collaborative pairing—that is, close collegial relationships between individuals across organizations, based on roles, interests, and personalities. These relationships enabled individuals to come together to accomplish common or highly interdependent tasks. In effect, these collaborative pairings represented a linking of role-related counterparts in the different collaborating organizations. There were several such pairings in these projects formed around different tasks.

The pairing of Joan with Beverly was particularly significant in the CMC project. Together they accomplished many of the day-to-day tasks involved in the development and implementation of the program at CMC, and they were jointly responsible for overall project management. The pairing of Joan and Derek was also critical to the success of the CMC project. Until Derek was assigned to the project, Joan had no one at Northland with whom to work to resolve the initial tensions between the two partner organizations. Things went much more smoothly after Derek came on board, and he and Joan formed a strong working relationship. In the Prairie College project, the pairing of "Dr. Deere" at the college with Dave at Deere helped to resolve issues related to the availability of equipment, parts, and tools, among other issues.

The basis for these pairings seems to have been similar roles and task-related interests. The pairing of Joan and Beverly came about because they were counterparts in the different organizations they represented; it was not based on any communality of personality or background, which, as we have seen, was minimal at best. Rather, Joan and Beverly were thrown together because they had similar responsibilities and joint tasks. In effect, they had to pair off in order for the project to work. In addition, because the participants in each project were in the same geographical area, the liaisons often met face to face early in the project, thereby developing the strong relationships that were the foundation of their collaboration. It was also fortunate that they had other qualities—for example, the afore-mentioned lateral skills—that enabled them to work together so effectively. These skills smoothed the way so that the people in liaison roles could work together on their common tasks despite obvious differences in personality and background.

All the collaborative pairings in these two projects occurred at the operational level, between team members engaged in the on-going, everyday tasks required to execute project goals. Pairings at higher levels, especially between the executive sponsors within each organization involved in the project, might also have helped. Consider, for example, how a collegial, person-to-person relationship between executive sponsors at ABC and Northland might have eased the uncertainty concerning the latter company's continued involvement in the project after its first representative left in the first few months.

In summary, the prominence and the significance of these collaborative pairings in both projects suggest that all organizations involved in complex collaborations of this sort need to enable the formation of such pairings by creating liaison roles, putting people in these roles who have good lateral skills, and creating the opportunity for them to form strong relationships with each other through face-to-face interactions. These pairings should also be created between project sponsors, to provide escalation paths for resolving issues that cannot be effectively addressed by those involved in the day-to-day details of the project.

Phase III: Creating the Infrastructure

In simple collaborations with few collaborators, straightforward challenges, and interactions that are frequent and direct—as in a small group whose members have face-to-face contact—teams can get by with minimal predetermined formal structure, and team members can work out issues concerning roles, responsibilities, and processes as they arise. Informality and spontaneity are not only possible but desirable. Complex collaborations, by contrast, have to deal with challenges of size, distance, cultural differences, and organizational boundaries. Therefore, they need structure in order to keep chaos to a minimum. Designing the appropriate structure is one of the first challenges that should be addressed in a complex, multiorganizational project. The John Deere projects illustrate this point well, both in terms of what they did and in terms of important issues they happened to overlook.

Create a Structure for Governance and Authority

One of the first tasks undertaken in both projects was the creation of a governance and authority structure to manage, conduct, and oversee the project. At the core of this structure were the advisory committee and the implementation team. The latter was never formally defined or named as such ("implementation team" is our expression, not the participants'), but there was a clear distinction between two groups of participants: a group of "doers" who were responsible for the day-to-day tasks, and an advisory committee, so named, whose function was as its name suggests.

The composition of the implementation team was fairly fluid; that is, the boundaries of this team were flexible, and they changed over time as team members moved from one set of tasks to another. For example, Myra Holt, ABC's training director, who worked with Don Garnet to get the program started, was initially a very important member of the CMC implementation team. After Joan joined ABC and gained enough familiarity and experience to take over Myra's responsibilities, Myra played a less active role in the project. Others also took on critical roles when their efforts were needed, and they moved to the periphery of the project or left entirely once their immediate help was no longer required. Despite this frequently changing, ad hoc membership, there was a stable core— Joan, Beverly, Don, Derek, and Mick—that persisted more or less throughout the critical early months of the project. There was a similar group with similar properties in the Prairie College project.

In both projects, the members of the implementation team also participated as members of the advisory committee. This group was larger and included representatives from all the dealer stores involved in the project, local representatives from Deere, and other peripheral but important people (for example, senior administrators at the colleges). Its purpose was to give advice on the development of the training program, recruit students, and provide the equipment, tools, and parts that students would work with in the hands-on portion of their training. In neither project did the participants formally differentiate between the implementation team and the advisory committee. As a result, there was some ambiguity, reflected in the interviews and project documents, about the definition and membership of the two teams.

The participants' approach to leadership mirrored their informal approach to team definition—that is, just as the implementation teams were never formally designated as such, neither were the leaders. The leadership role was just another one to be filled, and different individuals filled it as needed, depending on the issues to be addressed. There was no formally designated leader or "boss" assigning tasks and responsibilities to the other team members. Instead, different individuals or collaborating pairs of individuals would step up to the plate, as it were, and take on whatever needed to be done at a particular time. Decisions about who would do what seemed to emerge from discussions, in meetings and elsewhere, instead of being handed down by people in positions of formal authority on the teams.

Even though a formal project leader was never designated as such, this role was apparently covered quite effectively by a combination of factors. To begin with, the role was shared among the representatives of the participating organizations. Perhaps this informal, ad hoc approach would not work as well in other projects, but the flexibility afforded by shared leadership enabled the teams to accommodate the changing needs of the two projects. In addition, Mick and Joan, the representatives from the only organizations involved in both projects, provided continuity throughout the critical first year of the projects. Finally, all the participants were facilitative and collegial in how they dealt with their leadership roles, and that was probably the only approach that could have worked in such a multiorganizational collaboration, where the organizations were essentially equal partners.

That said, it should be noted that one individual, Mick Sims, consistently played a leadership role in the overall program and in the two projects. He was the one who had created the program—in effect, it was his baby—and he approached his role with drive and passion. He was intensely involved in the development of all the projects and was very involved when he had to be. Of course, this is just what was needed to get the program started and to expand it nationwide. But as the economy changed and Deere's priorities shifted, Mick was replaced with Richard Park. The goal then switched to maintaining the current programs, without adding any new ones, and to putting more responsibility for project leadership on the dealers. Therefore, Richard's role became more advisory, and the amount of his time that was devoted to the program—approximately 10 percent, compared to Mick's almost 80 percent—reflects this change in strategy and focus.

In summary, it appears that leadership should be shared in interorganizational collaborations among essentially equal partners, with different individuals taking on different tasks according to the skills, expertise, and influence required for those tasks. Regardless of who takes the lead on particular tasks at particular times, the style of leadership needs to be facilitative and collegial. Nevertheless, someone does need to drive the project in its early stages, to get it started and keep it going. This person should probably be the representative from the organization initiating the project. But as we have seen in the case of the Deere C&F Tech Program, conditions and priorities change, and so there must be flexibility in who fills the leadership role and in how it is defined and carried out. Different stages, conditions, and purposes may very well require different approaches, styles, roles, and people.

Formalize Roles, Relationships, and Understandings

Lack of fixed clarity about team membership and project leadership seemed to present no problem in the two projects, but a similar lack of clarity about other roles, responsibilities, and expectations apparently did. For example, as already mentioned, the number of different dealerships involved in the Prairie College project caused some confusion at the beginning, especially for the participants from the college. It took them some time to sort out all the players, the parties whom they represented, and their respective roles. Although this was not a serious problem, trying to find out who had to be contacted for equipment, tools, answers, and so on, did slow things down a bit in the beginning. It was not just that actors, roles, and relationships were not clearly defined. Even if all of it had been clearly laid out from the beginning, the Prairie College participants would still have preferred a simpler structure, a more centralized one, with a single contact person to whom they could have gone for most of their needs. Once Dave Harsha of Deere was put in this role, however, the Prairie College participants' concerns were essentially alleviated.

This suggests that formal, specific, and widely shared role definitions might not have been enough if the roles and structure they defined had been too complex. In other words, they needed clarity *plus* simplicity to begin collaborating effectively on the project tasks. This issue, in and of itself, is not likely to bring down a project marked by good intentions, shared goals, and committed participants, as were both of the projects described here. Lack of a clear, simple, and appropriate structure, however, when combined with the many other things that can and often do go wrong, can be very serious indeed.

Greater clarity and formalized understandings would also have helped in dealing with some of the early difficulties between ABC and Northland or possibly would even have prevented them entirely. As we noted earlier, when several employees left ABC to take jobs at Northland, Joan and others at ABC feared that this might be an intimation of a future problem: students supported by ABC taking jobs with Northland after their graduation from the program. If something like the "gentleman's agreement" between Joan and Derek had been developed and formalized earlier, it might have reduced the tensions and enabled the project to get off to a faster and smoother start. All of this suggests that an explicit contract, a charter, or some other form of documentation is essential for clearly defining the roles, responsibilities, expectations, and understandings that are critical to the project's success.

Both projects used a number of documents—letters of agreement attached as an appendix to the proposal to the Minnesota Job Skills Program, program brochures listing responsibilities of the different organizations, and so on—to address many of the issues that a formal contract might have covered in an interorganizational collaboration such as this one. As thoughtful and thorough as these documents were, both projects would have benefited from a more formal agreement or charter developed by all the parties at the earliest stages of the project. The proposals and brochures were essentially developed in reaction to particular issues or needs, not in anticipation of potential problems.

In summary, some kind of explicit agreement, contract, formal understanding, or charter is necessary in interorganizational collaborations where sensitive boundary issues can inhibit the development of trust and the open exchange of information and ideas. If collaborators rely on external circumstances and requirements, such as those imposed by funding agencies, to shape formal agreements and understandings, these agreements may include only those issues that are important to the external parties or agencies, missing other issues that may be even more critical to the projects' success. It is better for collaborators to take the bull by the horns early on and deal with these issues among themselves. That way, they can ensure that the issues that are most important to them are addressed and not left to be dealt with later, after they erupt and threaten the project.

Before we leave this topic, it is important to note that the processes for generating these agreements may be as useful as the agreements themselves. As we have noted elsewhere, the creative tension inherent in the collaborative process can be both messy and productive. This means that collaborators need to uncover and reconcile their frequently divergent viewpoints, positions, and goals. Conflict and tension are inevitable in these new working relationships, but if a conflict is managed well, compromises will emerge that are more creative and productive (Mankin, Cohen, and Bikson, 1996, p. 12). Furthermore, the working relationships created by the process will be much stronger than the paper on which these agreements eventually are written.

Phase IV: Doing the Work

After their early efforts to get these two projects off on a sound footing, the participants in both spent most of their time developing the programs, recruiting students, and dealing with the day-to-day challenges of managing a new educational program. Two sets of activities were especially prominent during this last phase of the projects. The first had to do with the primary means used by the participants to work together in executing their tasks and carrying out their responsibilities. The second reflected their response to the constraints imposed by the changing economic conditions that ultimately limited their achievements. What they did in response to these constraints is not typical for projects of this sort, and so it offers an excellent object lesson on the importance of learning from doing and snatching modest success from the jaws of defeat when that is all that can reasonably be achieved.

Meet and Communicate Frequently

Frequent communications and meetings played an important role in both projects. Early on, the participants recognized the importance of face-to-face meetings to develop personal relationships and build trust. They also used face-to-face meetings periodically throughout the projects to reinforce these relationships and, as necessary, to deal with particularly sensitive issues. Despite the regional concentration of each project, however, distances were just too great, and time was too scarce, to address all needs through face-to-face meetings. Therefore, once the projects were under way, the participants held phone conferences every four to six weeks to conduct most of their business.

The members of the implementation teams also used the phone and e-mail to communicate frequently between face-to-face meetings and scheduled phone conferences. Much of this more informal interaction took place in the collaborative pairs described earlier, or in small ad hoc groups composed of both implementation team and advisory committee members that emerged around particular tasks and issues. In the early stages of the CMC project, for example, Joan and Beverly talked almost every day, mostly by phone.

Members of the project teams also communicated frequently with others in their organizations, such as key managers and executives, who were not directly involved in the projects but were nevertheless important to overall success. This kind of communication was conducted primarily via e-mail. All the organizations except Deere are relatively small and geographically concentrated, and so informal and spontaneous face-to-face interactions also helped keep everyone informed. For example, Joan's office at ABC was next to Myra's and just down the hall from the CEO's, and so Joan could often bring the other two up to date when she ran into them in the hallways. Other complex collaborations, especially those involving larger and more dispersed organizations, cannot always count on such serendipitous channels of communication and may have to rely instead on more formal, intentional methods (for example, periodic e-mail progress reports).

All these means—face-to-face meetings, phone conferences, and more informal communications—are critical elements of an overall process of frequent interaction that uses whatever channels are available and appropriate for the issues to be addressed. It is also important to note that in these two projects, but especially in the one at CMC, the strength of the participants' relationships made it possible for them to use such a wide variety of means for meetings and informal communications. Projects in which relationships are less amicable require more frequent and more formal face-to-face meetings. The conclusion from this and related research and experience is that good relationships can support communications media that are less personal and more varied (see, for example, Sproul and Kiesler, 1991).

Learn from Doing and Adapt

As we saw earlier, the projects were only partially successful. The programs were implemented, students did enter the programs, and, by all accounts, they received the kind of training they needed to progress rapidly in their new careers. From the beginning, however, the number of students was well below what was expected and needed. As a result, both programs have undergone significant changes. The CMC program has merged with other, similar programs offered by Central Minnesota College, and the program in central Texas, after shutting down at Prairie College, moved to another college in the same region.

These developments, rather than indicating failed action or inaction, demonstrate effective responses to changing conditions and priorities. When the program began, the economy was strong, service technicians were in short supply, and the dealers had to cope every day with the impact of these shortages. After two years, however, the economy slowed and the shortage disappeared, at least from the everyday experience of the dealers. This issue was no longer as high a priority for them. Their recruiting efforts dropped off, and enrollments suffered as a result. At this point, Deere and the colleges also reconsidered the level and nature of their involvement, and they revised their goals, expectations, and plans accordingly.

In a nutshell, this is why the programs failed to achieve their long-term goals, despite their apparent short-term successes. By no means, however, should these programs' experience be defined as a failure, nor should any of the organizations be faulted for what they did or did not do. Conditions changed—that is inevitable in any long-term program or project. In this situation, failure would have been to single-mindedly stick with the original plans when everything clearly indicated that the original goals were no longer feasible. Other priorities emerged to compete for the attentions of the participating organizations, and so goals were revised and plans were adapted to the new realities. If success is defined by the ability to adapt to changing conditions and priorities, then the programs were successful even though they did not fully succeed in achieving their original goals.

These conditions, and the participants' responses to them, illustrate two very important action steps for any complex collaboration involving a long-term, noncritical project that is subject to changing circumstances not under the control of the collaborating organizations. First, the participants in these two projects regularly engaged in learning processes that helped them monitor their progress and learn from what was working and what was not. For example, the annual meeting of all the instructors in the various programs, which was primarily intended to bring the instructors up to speed on the latest innovations in Deere equipment and service technology, was also used to share ideas and experiences about the curriculum, the course content, and teaching techniques. In addition, both of the Deere-based directors, Mick Sims and Richard Park, served an important learning function by traveling around from one school to another, sharing what they had learned from working with the different programs under Deere's C&F Tech umbrella.

But the most important learnings emerged from the discussions that Richard had with the advisory committees, with other contacts at the participating organizations, and with his colleagues and the management team at Deere. These discussions made it clear that the original goals of the program were just too ambitious, especially in the face of the slowing economy. Without these discussions and the decisions and strategic choices that followed, the participants might have spent many more months of fruitless effort and frustration in the pursuit of unattainable goals.

Significant modifications to the programs have now been made, to adapt them to the constraints imposed by the economy and by the nature of C&F Tech Program itself. This suggests one last action step that should apply to all complex collaborations, regardless of type, purpose, or conditions: program and project goals and plans must be adapted to changing conditions and to what has been learned. Adaptable goals and plans are a critical success factor for almost any project, and this is especially true for complex, long-term collaborations subject to external factors outside the participants' control. This may be the most important success factor of all in terms of what it takes to keep a program like this going and ultimately achieve the only kind of success that is reasonably attainable.

Chapter Three

Across Time, Distance, and Culture

The Case of Radica Games Group, Inc.

The case presented in this chapter is similar to the last case in that it also consists of two projects. That is where the similarity ends. A first difference involves the nature of the projects that comprise the two cases—specifically, the development of new products, as described in this chapter, by contrast with the development of training programs, as described in the previous chapter. A second difference is captured by the distinction between the old and the new economy. Despite the dated, overdone, and misleading nature of this distinction, it is useful here as a metaphor for the very different "flavors" of the two cases. Whereas the John Deere case fits all the stereotypes of the old economy—the construction equipment industry in the midwestern region of the United States—this case is somewhat more geared to the new economy in its history, structure, process, and product.

The most important difference between the two cases concerns the nature and the structure of the complex collaboration described in each case. The case of the Radica Games Group, Inc., described in this chapter, involves only one organization, not several. One should not assume, however, that this case is therefore less complex than the previous one. In several important respects, it is actually far more complex. The projects described in this chapter involve collaborations across such far-flung locations as London, Dallas, Hong Kong, and Dongguan City in the People's Republic of China. This international collaboration has had to overcome the challenges of different time zones, different cultures, and different languages, and some of these challenges manifested in very unexpected ways. Therefore, even though all of this played out within the boundaries of only one organization, if we had to order our cases along a dimension of complexity, this one would be more complex than the last case, lying somewhere near the middle of the scale.

About Radica

The Radica Games Group is one of the world's leading manufacturers of electronic games, including handheld and tabletop games, high-tech toys, and video game controllers and peripherals. The company started out in 1983 as a small operation in Hong Kong, manufacturing gaming devices and souvenir casino games for the Las Vegas market. It later expanded its product line to include electronic versions of these games, when the company opened a factory in southern China in 1991 and a marketing and distribution operation in the United States in 1992. The business grew rapidly from that point on and soon became the leading supplier of casino-style electronic games in the United States, with such games as video poker and video blackjack. Anticipating a decline in the market for these games, Radica began to diversify its product line in 1995 to include other electronic handheld and tabletop games. The product that eventually transformed the company from a small, struggling operation into an industry leader was the Bass Fishin' game, the first project to be described in this chapter.

The first in a line of electronic fishing games, this product revolutionized the category of electronic handheld games. The product itself is in the shape of the handle end of a fishing rod and reel, and it features motion-sensing technology that simulates the actual kinesthetic and tactile experience of fishing. According to a description on the company's Web site, "the player casts, feels the fish bite, sets the hook with a jerk, and reels in the fish with a real handle." The Web site also notes that "the product started an industry trend in creating virtual reality games where the product provides the feel of the real sport." Radica's most recent products employing this principle include a line of Tiger Woods golf games, a virtual snowboard game that the user actually rides, and a virtual motorcycle game that "looks like a real motorcycle handlebars and gas tank, steers with motion sensing technology and shakes when you hit a road obstacle." The company's slogan aptly conveys the important role of virtual motion in these games: "Get real . . . get Radica."

In 1999 Radica acquired Leda Media Products, a manufacturer of video game controllers in the U.K., so that Radica could enter this rapidly expanding market. This market has been driven in recent years by the growing popularity of video game consoles produced by such giants of consumer electronics as Nintendo, Sony, and, now, Microsoft. Controllers are handheld devices that plug into the video game consoles and are the means by which users play the game. Radica is now producing game controllers for the Sony PlayStation, the Nintendo GameCube, and Microsoft's Xbox. The development of these new products is the focus of the second project described in this chapter.

Radica currently employs about four thousand people in its offices in the United Kingdom, the United States, and Hong Kong and in its factory in southern China. The U.K. and U.S. sites have primary responsibility for "ideation" (ideas for games, and the initial design of game flow and features), product design, and marketing; Hong Kong does engineering design; and the factory in China does the manufacturing. The responsibilities of the different sites have begun to overlap in recent years as these sites, particularly Hong Kong and China, have developed new skills and capabilities. For example, some engineering design is now done at the China factory. But, for the most part, the sorting of tasks and responsibilities by site continues and is one of the primary ways in which the company deals with the profound challenges of great distance, different time zones, and dramatically diverse cultures and languages.

The Bass Fishin' Game Project

Long before the ideas underlying this game were hatched, two employees were laying the foundations for its future success, as well as for the future success of the entire company. One was Bob Davids, a consultant to the company in its earliest years, who became CEO in 1988. The other was S. W. Lam, a young industrial engineer from Hong Kong who joined the company in 1985. Their different backgrounds, complementary values, and the especially strong relationship that developed between them in the early years of the company helped to shape Radica's organizational culture for many years to come.

Background and History

Bob grew up in the vibrant custom-car culture of early 1960s Los Angeles. His early exposure to this culture led to an enduring interest in the design arts, an interest that was later reinforced during his college years at the cutting-edge Art Center College of Design in Pasadena. After graduating as an industrial designer, he worked for a few years as the manager of a casino in Reno, Nevada, then started consulting to Radica shortly after it was founded in 1985. He became a co-owner a year later and moved to Hong Kong to take over as CEO in 1988.

Lam's background is quite different. He grew up in Hong Kong and studied industrial and production engineering at the Hong Kong Polytechnic University. Like many young, creative Chinese raised in Hong Kong during the years when it was a British colony, he was exposed to and greatly influenced by Western culture. The rich stew of Western and Asian culture that characterized Hong Kong during Lam's formative years led to his abiding interest in the blending of Western and Asian values and to ideas for creating business organizations that take advantage of the best that each culture has to offer. Lam's interest in military strategy also contributed to his developing ideas about leadership and organization.

His partnership with Bob began after Bob became CEO. One of their first projects was to change the work week from five and a half days to five so that the workers could return refreshed to work on Monday and, in Bob's words, "compete against the world." This was more difficult than it would seem, since the Hong Kong workers were suspicious about Bob's motives and about what they would have to give up in return.

Lam was also skeptical at first. He was afraid that shortening the work week would make Radica less competitive. But he supported Bob's efforts because Bob "was the boss and could do whatever he wanted." Lam's role as a "crossover point between the two cultures" was critical to the ultimate success of this project. He was able to convince the managers and workers at the plant, all of whom were Chinese, that their American boss was well-intentioned, wanted to do what was in their best interests, and was not trying to exploit them.

The change effort was successful. Productivity increased, and, apparently, so did employee satisfaction. The impressive results and Lam's growing respect for Bob's judgment and values convinced Lam that Bob's "radical" ideas could work at Radica. The experience also reinforced Lam's initial impression that Bob was genuinely sincere in his respect for the employees. He could see that Bob "had a good heart," was "fair," and, unlike many other Westerners in Hong Kong in those days, was not condescending and patronizing toward the Chinese workers. Lam and Bob also had several qualities in common, which helped to strengthen their rapidly developing relationship. They are both "engineers" (as noted earlier, Bob was actually an industrial designer, and industrial design is fairly close in spirit to engineering at its most creative). They are also self-described workaholics, principled, and very tenacious. Furthermore, both are strong believers in the values of "humility, honesty, respect, and trust." Their mutual respect, shared values, and similar work styles solidified their working relationship.

Bob and Lam continued to work closely together for several more years to create a company culture that contrasted in many ways with the national culture that surrounded them. Perhaps the biggest challenge was empowering the workers in the factory in China. Neither the managers nor the workers were initially recep-tive to the idea of worker empowerment. The managers were used to giving directions, and the workers were used to following them. The workers' attitude was "If I'm doing your job and making deci-sions, I should be getting your salary."

It took at least six years before the workers were willing to ac-cept some degree of responsibility for making decisions, and it was somewhat longer than that before the managers in the plant stopped resisting this new reality. Bob's persistence, sincerity, and hands-on attitude had finally paid off, but it was Lam's ability to bridge the cultures that ultimately made the difference. And it was their relationship, highly visible to everyone involved, that pro-vided the model for how to adapt the traditional Chinese culture to the new world of international collaboration. This unique rela-tionship would soon serve as the foundation for the project that would transform the company and for the culture that helps drive its success even today.

The next step in the transformation of the company, and in the ongoing evolution of Lam's role, was Bob's decision to create a product design group in the United States. This decision reflected Bob's growing interest in developing games for the U.S. market and his belief that "design should be close to the market." Besides, the United States had an abundance of experience, expertise, and cre-ativity in product design and marketing. The design group was created in 1993 and was located at the Radica sales and marketing offices in the suburbs of Dallas.

By now Bob could see that Lam had "one foot in each culture." He took advantage of Lam's boundary-spanning talents, sending him to the United States to represent engineering in the product design group as well as "to teach Americans how to save money." Lam's title and role changed as a result. In Hong Kong he had been manager of engineering design and was primarily concerned with issues of technical production. In Dallas he was director of engineering and was now responsible for managing design projects.

Despite Bob's and Lam's largely successful efforts to transform the company, Radica nearly went bankrupt in 1995. The sales and profitability of the company's primary product line, casino games, were topping out, and other companies were now competing with Radica in an increasingly limited market. It was time for Radica to live up to its name and come up with new, radically different product lines. Therefore, the company began to explore possibilities for the next generation of Radica games.

Bob felt that Radica's next best opportunity for new electronic games was in the world of sports. It was perhaps no coincidence that Bob's other passion, aside from the company he had led for the previous several years, was fishing. His hobby—the second most popular participant sport in North America (bowling is first)—became his inspiration. Why not create a fishing game that captured the essence of fishing, a game that would represent and convey to the player the very features that attracted Bob and millions of other people around the world to this challenging, frequently frustrating, and often rewarding sport?

Bob wanted to put these features into a game with "high play value," a game that consumers would view as more than just a "cheap throw-away Christmas toy." The product that emerged from this project was not just an abstract, digital representation of the decision-making process involved in fishing (for example, choosing lures and picking the best fishing spots to cast a line). Even more important was that the game should also convey the physical "feel" of fishing, including the motions of casting and reeling. Thus was born the virtual-motion concept behind the Bass Fishin' game, one of the most successful handheld electronic games in the history of the industry.

Because of this game, the product line that grew out of it, and the other products based on the virtual-motion concept that Radica developed over the next several years, Radica went through a dramatic turnaround, going from the edge of bankruptcy in 1995 to a profit of $50 million within two years after the release of the first version of the game. How they executed this turnaround is the story of the project behind the success of the Bass Fishin' game.

The Project Team

The structure and membership of the project team reflected the process by which the product was designed, developed, and manufactured. The process was divided into key tasks, broadly defined, and each task was assigned to a team at the regional site best suited to execute it.

Ideation in Dallas. The first task in the process was ideation and product design. This included deciding on the features of the game, the game flow (that is, the sequence of decisions and actions that make up the total game experience), and the game's look and feel. The product design group at Radica's Dallas office was assigned responsibility for this task. The group was made up of Bob and Lam, several industrial designers, and the design supervisor, Kevin Brase. This core group remained fairly intact throughout most of the project and was supplemented at various times by other designers, but the team's total size held fairly constant at six or seven members, including Bob.

Radica did not have a marketing department at the time, but Bob's industry experience as an executive and, perhaps most important, his experience as a fisherman enabled him to provide the marketing expertise that the team needed. In effect, he served as a surrogate customer for the team. There was a sales department, but its members were initially pessimistic about the prospects for the game, and so they were not actively involved in its design and development. (It should be noted, however, that they did an excellent job of selling the game to retailers when it finally came out.)

As the project moved forward, Bob became less and less involved in the day-to-day activities of the project team, although he continued to play an important leadership and facilitative role in the project (we will have more to say about Bob and Lam's leadership role). The nitty-gritty work of the team was left to the designers. From their ongoing collaboration emerged the innovative features that helped re-create the physical essence of fishing—the earliest manifestation of the virtual-motion concept that would define Radica games for years to come.

We interviewed all the members of the Dallas team who were still with the company at the time of our research, and they were unanimous in their almost nostalgic recollections of how the team had worked. The camaraderie among the team members had been high, fueled in part by the go-for-broke nature of the project as well as by the skepticism expressed by the sales department and others at Radica. Memories of the project were clearly treasured by the team members as belonging to a particular moment in time, to a special period in the evolution of a small company, when goals were more straightforward and pathways less complex. Kevin Brase remembers the team as "small, very entrepreneurial and informal. . . . We had an idea and just ran with it. . . . There were few obstacles other than time. There was nothing to get in the way."

Engineering in Hong Kong, Manufacturing in China. The second task, the software engineering and electromechanical design of the game itself, was assigned to the engineers in Hong Kong because of their expertise in engineering design. Bob was also impressed by the work ethic, attention to detail, and focus on costs that characterized most of the engineers with whom he had come in contact in Radica's early years in Hong Kong. The manufacturing was done in the factory in China, primarily because of the significantly lower labor costs in China, but Bob was also interested in taking advantage of the Chinese "creativity in tooling and production," as he put it, and especially of how they were able to translate this creativity into efficient, low-cost manufacturing.

The team in Hong Kong was made up of three core members, who were on board throughout most of the project, plus a couple of additional engineers at different points in the project. The plant manager and the manufacturing engineer from the factory in China worked closely with the team in Hong Kong. Because the factory is only about forty miles from the offices in Hong Kong, the Hong Kong engineers were often able to travel to the factory, but the border crossing between China and the Hong Kong territories (now designated a "special administrative region" by the Chinese government) made this trip longer and more inconvenient than the actual distance might otherwise suggest.

Our interviews with the Hong Kong team members were conducted in English, their second or even third language, and so these subjects were not as effusive in their recollections of the project as their Dallas counterparts were. Perhaps, too, the Hong Kong cohort was culturally more reserved than their colleagues in Texas. In any case, the feelings and experiences they shared were just as positive, especially in their descriptions of how they had communicated and worked with the team in Dallas. (We will have more to say about this issue.)

Project Leadership. As in the John Deere case, leadership of the project team was shared. At least three members took on critical leadership functions throughout the project. Bob, as the CEO and the person who had initiated the project, played several leadership roles. The only one on the team who knew how to fish, he was the team's subject-matter expert, the person who knew the most about the activity that the game was supposed to simulate. In this role he helped the team translate abstract ideas about the experience of fishing into actual game features.

Another of Bob's roles derived from his background as an industrial designer and from the problem-solving focus that is the sine qua non of this profession. As he describes this role, he "painted the parameters and defined the problem for them, and they generated the solution." He saw his role as getting the other members of the team to think the way fishermen do: "What does a bass fisherman do when he gets up in the morning? What are the things he thinks about: where should I go to fish, what's the weather, what tackle should I use?" Bob also supervised the design reviews, making sure that the game struck the right balance, including enough features to offer high play value but not so many as to raise its price out of the reach of Radica's typical customer.

Yet another of Bob's roles was a symbolic one. Because he had been responsible for creating Radica's culture of openness and mutual trust and respect, his very presence reminded the other participants of the values guiding their interactions with each other, and with others outside the team. He also facilitated the team's processes, to make sure that they reflected these values. He encouraged open discussion and made sure that all the participants were respected for their expertise and experience, for what they had to contribute. Bob constantly urged the others to express their views and question his positions, but he was also prepared to step in when the team was unable to make a decision or resolve a dispute.

Several of Bob's roles can be seen in action in the decision about how challenging the game should be—in other words, how long it would take the average player to catch a fish. The trade-off was between realism and fun. In real life it can take thirty minutes or longer to catch a fish, but few people other than experienced fishermen have the patience to play a game with such a miserly payoff. The team had to decide whether the game would be marketed to experienced fishermen or to novices. After much indecision, Bob stepped in to resolve the issue in favor of novices. It took several more months of trial and error to finally get the right balance between a game that was challenging enough to be rewarding but easy enough to keep players interested.

Lam's role on the team was very different but complementary to Bob's roles. Lam often served as a foil for Bob, questioning his positions before decisions were made, a role that Bob especially valued and encouraged. In addition, Lam had primary responsibility for pricing. He could discard features that others had designed into the game if those features threatened to price the game out of its market. He also conducted interviews with some of Bob's friends who were bass fishermen and arranged fishing trips for his designers, to help them come up with more realistic designs for the game.

Probably Lam's most important role was to bridge the different cultures involved in the project: the cultures of the United States and Hong Kong, but also the creative culture of the design team and the more pragmatic culture of the engineering and production teams. In this role, Lam was able to serve as an information channel between Asia and the United States, letting everybody know what was happening at the other sites and, as he put it, "communicating with all critical parties about critical issues." He appreciated the designers' desire to make the game as imaginative and realistic as possible, but he also understood the engineering and production constraints in Hong Kong and China. More than once he had to tell his colleagues in Dallas, "We can't do this because we don't have the machine in China that can do it."

Because of Lam's success in this role, he was trusted by all parties. In addition, one of the Hong Kong engineers noted that Lam worked "sincerely" in his job and that he led by example in his "planning and caring." Furthermore, Bob and Lam together provided a good model of East-West collaboration, and their very obvious commitment to the project made it clear to everyone involved just how important the project was.

Kevin also played an important leadership role. As design manager, he supervised the other product designers on the team: tracking tasks, conducting performance reviews, answering questions for the other designers, and so on. In sum, Bob posed the challenge and the approach, Lam represented the engineering and manufacturing constraints to the design team, and Kevin supervised the designers. Other team members also stepped in as they were needed to play leadership roles in the project, particularly when their specialized expertise fit the particular design challenges of the moment. All the team members we interviewed felt that they had important roles in the project's success and that their contributions were highly valued by Bob, Lam, and everyone else involved in the project.

The Process

The product development process, as described earlier, was designed to take advantage of the relative strengths of each culture—the marketing and product design capabilities of the Americans, and the engineering and low-cost manufacturing skills of the Chinese. That meant that there were two distinct teams—the design team in the United States, and the engineering team in Hong Kong. The factory in China was in effect a third team, with a different purpose (that is, production). The factory workers also spoke a dialect, Mandarin, that was different from the Cantonese used in Hong Kong, and they had a different culture as well (the Hong Kong culture was more business-oriented, aggressive, entrepreneurial, and "Western" than the socialist culture of the People's Republic of China). Because of the two groups' geographical and functional proximity, the group in Hong Kong had to interact closely with the factory in China and sometimes acted as a liaison between the designers in the United States and the factory. To overcome the language differences, all the Hong Kong engineers learned to speak at least some Mandarin.

The nature of the product created new challenges for Radica. As a completely new kind of game for Radica, it required the designers in Dallas, the engineers in Hong Kong, and the factory in China to work very closely together. The very nature of the new product created an additional problem as well. As noted earlier, it was the first product of its kind to involve virtual motion and physical action. The challenge was to turn the new, abstract ideas generated by the game designers in Dallas into programs and electromechanical designs in Hong Kong, and then into a virtual-motion product in China—all at a cost that would enable the company to sell enough games to generate a substantial profit.

By contrast with other electronic games, whose physical "feel" is secondary to the game actions embedded in electronic circuitry, the success of this new product depended on the game's ability to simulate the kinesthetic and tactile experience of fishing. The only way to check out the product, to make sure that it created the experience it was designed to create, was to look at it, pick it up, cast the "line," and reel in the virtual fish, fighting with it as it twisted and bucked at the end of the line. If the game was not successful in recreating the sensation of actually catching and reeling in a fish, it would not do well in the marketplace.

But the designers, who were the team members best able to judge the realism of the game experience, were several thousand miles away from the engineering and production process. To make things even more difficult, Radica was barely getting by. The company was facing increased competition for its gambling games, and the U.S. economy was only slowly emerging from a long recession. As a result, travel budgets were severely restricted. At the time, the company did not even have e-mail. Everyone had to rely on decidedly "old economy" communication systems—fax machines, telephones, and overnight express mail.

Communications. People used these older technologies and methods well, augmenting them with an incredible focus on tasks and outcomes, a determination to keep moving forward, considerable trust in each other's good intentions, capabilities, and judgment, and appropriate social norms and expectations about communications.

At the end of every workday, the product designers in Dallas faxed their drawings to the engineering team in Hong Kong. The drawings typically illustrated proposed features for the game or aspects of its physical appearance. The faxes were waiting for the engineers in Hong Kong when they arrived at work a couple of hours later. The engineers then had to decide whether they could execute and manufacture the designs within the limits of their target price point. If they felt that they could not, thought they had a better way, or had other issues and concerns, they countered with their own ideas, which they faxed back to Dallas by the end of their own workday. The U.S. team might push back, arguing that a particular feature was critical, and the dialogue might continue for a few iterations, but there was rarely any second-guessing once the Hong Kong engineers had made their limitations clear. The discussion ended, or other trade-offs between game features and costs were explored.

Physical mockups of the product, or "demoboards," as they were called, were also an important medium of communication. The mockups were essential to the product development process because they simulated the look and feel of the game. Without the mockups, the design team would have had little indication of how the development process was going until the product was actually in production—too late to make significant changes. The mockups were produced in Hong Kong or at the factory and then shipped to Dallas overnight. The design team then evaluated the mockups and faxed comments back, sometimes with design changes, if possible on the same day.

The difference in time zones acted both as an obstacle to and as a facilitator of collaboration. Because there is a thirteen-hour time difference, there was no overlap between the workday in Dallas and the workday in Hong Kong, and direct interaction between the two locations was difficult. In an excellent example of his dedication and hard work, Lam worked around this problem by talking on the phone in the evening with the engineers in Hong Kong whenever an issue arose that required real-time explanation or discussion. But the out-of-sync workdays also enabled the teams to work "around the clock," as they put it. With drawings faxed every evening from Dallas to Hong Kong, and feedback received when the Dallas design team returned to work the next morning, everyone was able to keep the work going, in a process that was much like the passing of a baton back and forth in a never-ending relay race.

On occasion Lam flew to Hong Kong to resolve difficult issues that required his presence either there or at the factory in southern China. On one such occasion, early in the project, a visit by Lam to the factory helped resolve a particularly vexing assembly problem in the initial pilot runs of the new product. While the Hong Kong engineers worked with the factory managers and engineers to solve the problem, Lam's presence provided critical psychological support and symbolized the concern and commitment of the highest levels of the company. In general, Bob and Lam traveled back and forth periodically to demonstrate their commitment to the project, keep everyone informed about what was going on, and give a face to the communications, designs, and decisions coming from the United States almost every day. Perhaps the most important outcome of these trips was reinforcement of the connections between the far-flung sites and of the mutual trust and respect that held everything together.

Mutual trust and respect were especially apparent in the care that the participants took in their communications with each other. Because of the foundations laid down by Bob and Lam over the preceding years, all those involved in the project were well aware of the role of culture in their communications and tried their best to minimize potential problems. The factor of different native languages, of course, was the most obvious manifestation of the communication challenges. As we noted earlier, there were three different native languages or dialects spoken at the three sites—English in Dallas, Cantonese in Hong Kong, and Mandarin at the factory in China. This presented quite a communications challenge for everyone involved. How they dealt with this challenge is discussed in Chapter Four.

Success . . . and New Challenges. The success of the product—one of the most popular games of its type in the history of the industry—transformed Radica from a small, struggling company with a limited product line into one of the powerhouses of today's electronic toy and game industry. But, like most other companies in today's fiercely competitive, rapidly changing global economy, Radica found that success can be fleeting. Radica's leaders recognized that they would not be able to rest on their laurels with the success of the Bass Fishin' game product line. It wasn't long before they started the innovation process again, this time with a new management team, a significantly restructured company, and an entirely new market and product line.

The Controller Projects

Several years after the success of the Bass Fishin' game and the other virtual-motion product lines that emerged from this revolutionary concept, Radica launched another project that would take the company in a significantly new direction. As a result, Radica is now a very different company from what it was at the beginning of the Bass Fishin' project. Therefore, many of the challenges that the company currently faces are different from those it faced in the earlier project, and we can learn much from Radica's experiences with these new challenges.

The company is much larger now and more complex. Bob Davids has left to spend more time fishing and to pursue a new business venture: a winery near Santa Barbara. Radica has a new CEO, Pat Feely, and he has a very different background—marketing, operations and finance—as well as extensive experience in the toy industry. His background and experience represent an important shift in the company and a focus on different issues.

Lam remained with the company through most of the controller projects (he has since left), but in a new position, that of executive vice president in charge of worldwide product development. In this role, he was less involved in day-to-day operations and instead played a more strategic role. For example, he oversaw research and development, a division that had not formally existed in the mid-1990s but is now one of Radica's most strategically important functions.

Many but not all of the original members of the Bass Fishin' game project team are still with the company, but generally not in the same positions. Although their culture of mutual respect was tested at times by the strains of growth and increased competition and by the challenges of integrating a new acquisition, mutual respect is still an important element of Radica's culture. Because of the more formal and complex nature of the company, however, mutual respect nowadays often takes a different, less personal form, as we will see.

The controller projects were still unfolding as this chapter was being written, and so we do not have the perspective of hindsight or ultimate outcomes to evaluate their success. The projects are far enough along, however, for some learnings and insights to have been gained. Given how difficult it is to capture the dynamic ambiguities of a project in progress, we will not try to pin down details but focus instead on how the controller projects are different from the Bass Fishin' game project and on how they are essentially the same.

The goal of these newer projects is to produce a line of hand-held devices (controllers), which are peripherals that plug into the video game consoles produced by Sony (PlayStation), Nintendo (GameCube), and Microsoft (Xbox). The consoles offer a wide variety of games, produced by the console manufacturers themselves or produced under contract or through licensing agreements with third parties. The controllers allow users to control the games, and they include game pads, steering wheels, memory cards, and other accessories. These products are very different from the toys and games that were Radica's mainstay in years past. It should not be surprising, then, that they have posed significant new challenges for the company.

New Complexities

The strategic importance of this new product line is obvious. The popularity of video games and video game consoles grows every year as new technological capabilities increase their sophistication and appeal. The market for the devices that control these games is almost as big as for the games themselves. It is easy to see why Radica has decided to move aggressively in this new direction, but to do so, the company had to develop new capabilities, and fast.

Pat Feely describes the reasoning behind this strategic move: "Radica's existing expertise in virtual reality technology for hand-held games applies well to video game control devices. That expertise is what led us in the direction of this much bigger and faster growing market segment." But what Radica lacked was a "market position," a known presence and distribution capability, especially in Europe, which was a potentially large and, for Radica, untapped market.

Like many other companies faced with the challenge of new markets, products, and capabilities, Radica chose to acquire a company that already had what they wanted rather than try to develop everything from scratch. In 1999, Radica acquired Leda Media Products (LMP), a British company that at the time of its acquisition was one of the leading developers and marketers of video game controllers in Europe. Both companies came to the table with something that the other one needed. LMP offered an established European sales and marketing capability as well as experience and visibility in the video game accessory market. Radica brought its track record of successful innovation, expertise in virtual-motion technology, and, perhaps most important of all for LMP, entry into the biggest market of all, North America. The hope on Radica's part was that this acquisition would accomplish more than just the addition of LMP's product and industry knowledge to Radica's design knowledge. What both companies were aiming for was a synergy between them, to create rich collaborations that would lead the now larger and more complex Radica into new, highly profitable directions.

It soon became clear, however, that this solution presented new challenges of its own. Solving one problem—limited product experience and access to the targeted market—the acquisition added to another: their ongoing challenges of collaboration across time, distance, and culture. As Feely has wryly noted about this larger and even more widely dispersed company, "The sun never sets on Radica." With the addition of LMP in the United Kingdom, the new Radica had to mesh the activities and cultures of four sites. Radica now had to face the same challenge as every other formerly small entrepreneurial organization that has been successful enough to survive its early years. The company had undergone considerable growth in the years since the Bass Fishin' game project, and the acquisition of LMP only added to its size and complexity. Radica had become too complex to be run as informally as had been done in the old days.

There was a certain irony to this new, more formal Radica, especially for the project team members in the United Kingdom. Before it was acquired by Radica, LMP had been small, entrepreneurial, and informal, just as Radica itself had been a few years earlier. But Radica was now a more mature company, and so the difference in culture between the new acquisition and the parent firm added yet another layer of complexity. The acquisition of the U.K. group added not only another node to the communication network and another step in the design process but also a new culture to be integrated. Cultural differences at Radica were now more than just an issue of geography and function.

To make things even more difficult for this larger, more complex Radica, market conditions for the new product line imposed new demands and constraints. Radica was competing not only with other companies like itself—that is, third-party manufacturers of controllers for video game consoles—but also with the manufacturers of the consoles themselves, especially Sony and Nintendo. These companies themselves produce the controllers to be used with their game consoles, and they typically sell them bundled with the consoles. As a result, they do not provide the specifications for their consoles to third-party manufacturers like Radica before the consoles are actually released on the market. Therefore, Radica can do little until then. Because the products are usually launched at different times in different markets (for example, first in Japan, and then in the United States and Europe), Radica has only four to eight months to move from ideation to a product that is ready when new Sony and Nintendo consoles first appear on the U.S. market.

Clearly, time is of the essence in this new market. Timing has always been important to Radica, but the development time had now become much shorter than it had ever been before, and it was under the control of the first-party manufacturers, not Radica. This has been a major change for Radica. In the past, Radica set the pace; now the pace is being set by others. LMP, the company that Radica acquired, was born in these market conditions and was therefore more familiar with the demands of this extremely short, externally driven product life cycle. Initially, however, the rest of Radica was not fully prepared for the increased pressure of this accelerated development cycle.

All of this—the increased complexity of the organization and of its new market—made the ongoing challenge of coordination across different sites in different time zones and countries even more difficult. The acquisition of LMP added yet another dimension to an organization that was already culturally and geographically complex. It should come as no surprise, then, that the new complexity and time pressures created new sources of conflict for Radica.

New Conflicts

Things did not go smoothly at first. The relatively congenial collaborative process that had developed over the previous years between the old partners in the United States and Hong Kong had to be reconfigured to accommodate the new partner. Not surprisingly, this change led to conflicts between the new and old partners.

Because the U.K. designers had the expertise and experience in the new market, Radica UK (as the new division was called) was put in the driver's seat for the controller projects. As a result, the U.K. team had to work directly with the engineers in Hong Kong. For the Hong Kong engineers, working with their new partners was very different from working with their old colleagues in Dallas. There was not the same long history of collaboration, and therefore not the same kind of relationship. Nor did the new partners in the United Kingdom have any history or experience with the Hong

Kong team, and so they had less reason to trust the engineers' capa-bilities than had the U.S. designers in years past. As a result, the U.K. designers did not always respond well when the Hong Kong engineers raised concerns or offered their own ideas, as they had done with the U.S. team during development of the Bass Fishin' game. Differences that had been quickly and creatively resolved between the U.S. and Hong Kong teams became conflicts between Hong Kong and the United Kingdom, often taking precious time and considerable effort to be worked out. More than once, the con-flicts required costly travel and production rework before they could be resolved. Time pressures turned up the heat under these conflicts and often made them more difficult than they had to be.

The decision to put Radica UK in charge also created conflict with the U.K. team's U.S. counterparts. Most of these conflicts were over branding strategy and the implications for brand name, prod-uct features, and packaging. The subtext, however, was clearly the new role of the "upstart" U.K. designers vis-à-vis that of the U.S. designers who were holdovers from an earlier, simpler time at Rad-ica. Management set the stage for the conflict by deciding that the basic product had to be "global"—that is, the controllers sold in the United States would be essentially identical to those sold in Europe. This decision enabled the company to keep production costs down by using common parts in the United States and Europe, and it helped Radica create a common brand identity and marketing strategy for consoles in both markets.

At first the U.S. division resisted the new arrangement. Pat Feely describes their attitude as initially dismissive: "We don't like anything they have, and we don't want to use their name, products, or packaging. We are going to do this our own way." According to Feely, U.S. companies throughout the industry were used to com-ing up with the ideas, creating the products, and "tossing them over the fence to the Europeans to do what they could with it. European divisions were basically forced to do whatever it was the Americans wanted." With Radica's decision to enter the new market and ac-quire LMP, the shoe was now on the other foot. This situation was made even more difficult by the U.S. division's justifiable pride in their legacy of creativity and their success with earlier Radica products, especially the Bass Fishin' game.

The U.K. designers, although they were essentially in charge, were not completely happy either, although for somewhat different reasons. They were not used to being merely a division of a larger organization. They felt that Radica was too hierarchical and slow. They chafed at what they saw as overly formal and bureaucratic processes for design review. Given a choice, many of them would still have been working on a local basis for a smaller company, with little need to accommodate other viewpoints and, from their perspective, compromise their designs as a result.

Logo Wars. Nothing illustrates the tension between the two new partners, and how they dealt with these conflicts, better than the battles over the logo for the expanding line of controller products. When Radica's leaders decided to go with a global product, they also elected to adopt LMP's name for it: namely, the Gamester brand of video game accessories, a brand identity that LMP had already established throughout Europe before being acquired by Radica. The existing Gamester logo was also chosen to be the common logo for all the products in the new global product line.

The U.S. designers, however, had their own ideas, not only about how the logo should look in general but particularly about the shape, colors, and features that would most appeal to U.S. consumers. They wanted to redesign the logo to match what they thought was most appropriate for the U.S. market. Several months of heated e-mails between the U.K. and U.S. designers led them dangerously close to an unacceptable solution: two logos, the existing one for the European market and a new one for the U.S. market. All of this conflict was taking far too long to resolve, especially given the time pressures imposed by the console manufacturers' product release strategy. The product had to ship by a certain date, and the designers were nowhere near over their stalemate, which by now had become even more difficult to resolve.

Good old-fashioned face-to-face relationship building finally saved the day. The relationship between several key senior managers—Jeanne Olsen, senior vice president of marketing in the United States, and her U.K. counterparts—laid the foundation for the conflict's resolution, which still took several months, spanning the transition from one U.K. division manager to another. Jeanne's strong working relationship with the first manager helped bring the feuding parties closer together. The equally strong relationship she quickly developed with his successor, John Doughty, finally closed the gap, when they were able to bring the principal warring parties together at a quarterly conference in Los Angeles.

Jeanne and John reaffirmed the earlier decision to go with the original shape of the Gamester logo, but they left the door open for some variations to accommodate different regional aesthetic preferences, without adding significantly to product cost. Because the shape of the logo was already embedded in the molds used to manufacture the controllers, altering the color of the logo and the packaging for the product was the most cost-effective way to express the differences between the U.S. and European products.

The two designers in charge of the project, one from the U.S. office and the other from the U.K. team—the principal combatants in the e-mail wars that had led up to this meeting—left the meeting together to work out the solution. Not only did they accomplish their aim in thirty minutes—they decided on stronger colors for the U.S. market and on boxes rather than "clamshells" for the European market—they were the best of friends by the end of the meeting. The tone of their e-mail interactions and the ease of their collaboration improved from that point on.

All the parties eventually survived the wars, worked out their differences, and emerged on the other side as effective partners with the strong relationships needed for long-term success. How did they do it? We will defer a more detailed answer to the next chapter, but one piece of the puzzle—communication—is worth discussing now because it was as much of a new challenge, in and of itself, as it was a partial solution to the problem.

New Communications Media . . . and More New Challenges

Communication was now more important than ever in pulling together this complex, often contentious collaboration. New forms of communication, and increased use of more familiar forms, played a key role in smoothing these conflicts but also created new ones.

Compared to the old Radica of the Bass Fishin' game era, the new, more geographically dispersed and culturally diverse Radica needed new forms of communication and used a variety of technology-based means to accomplish this. The designers and engineers, for example, instead of faxing designs and drawings every day between Dallas and Hong Kong as they had done several years before, now relied on a 3-D design software package called SolidWork, which links all four of the sites involved in design, engineering, and manufacturing. All design and engineering files are now sent electronically with this software. Nevertheless, the teams still use overnight express shipping to send models when designers or others need to make sure that a controller looks and feels right.

Probably the biggest change is that Radica now has e-mail and videoconferencing and makes frequent use of both. As a result, Radica now communicates more with text and words than before. This change may also reflect both the increased emphasis on marketing and the nature of the product itself. The nuances of different colors, packaging, and logos seem to produce more discussion and argument these days than in the past, fueled in part by the frequently different perspectives and opinions of the U.K. and U.S. teams.

E-mail is used extensively for these discussions, videoconferencing less so. Everyone views e-mail as an indispensable tool for integrating the different teams in widely different regions of the world, but there is also recognition of e-mail's limitations. Apparently the very technology that makes jobs easier can also make jobs more difficult. The issue once again is culture. Language differences associated with the different cultures, particularly between Asia and the West, are only a part of the communications challenge.

We have already seen how Radica dealt with the different cultures of the United States, Hong Kong, and China in the Bass Fishin' game project. One might think that the addition of the U.K. site should not have made much difference, given similarities in language and culture between the United States and the United Kingdom and even, to a certain degree, between the United Kingdom and Hong Kong. But the addition of the U.K. site led to unexpected communication problems, especially with respect to the role of humor in communication. International and comparative research over the years has consistently demonstrated that uses and interpretations of humor, and even formulations of what constitutes humor, can vary greatly from culture to culture (for example, see Erez and Earley, 1995). Differences in humor between the United States and the United Kingdom, on the one hand, and between these two cultures and the Chinese cultures, on the other (even the somewhat Westernized version of Chinese culture that exists in Hong Kong), have been particularly significant in Radica's experience. This was not unexpected, of course, but what was surprising were the differences in humor between the U.S. and U.K. teams.

E-mail seemed to exacerbate the problem. Studies have shown that e-mail communications tend to be abrupt, breezy, and informal, and to use a style rife with the potential for cross-cultural miscommunication (Sproul and Kiesler, 1991). Humor in particular can be difficult to convey by way of this "thin" medium. The ability to convey humor and the subtleties of irony in the one-dimensional, temporally drawn-out world of e-mail is hampered in the best of circumstances, and even more so in the context of the kinds of cultural differences that Radica had to deal with on a daily basis. Cultural differences in humor were less a factor in the Bass Fishin' game project, where communication was more visual, and more of a problem in the controller projects, where e-mail has been the primary means of communication, and where written messages rather than pictures have been the primary medium.

People at Radica also travel much more than they used to, for face-to-face meetings and for opportunities to check out the look and feel of their new products. The face-to-face meetings have helped build stronger relationships and have improved perceptions and attitudes among the sites. Face-to-face communications can also be misinterpreted, however, especially if the parties to the communication come from different cultures with widely different approaches to humor. For example, in a verbal conversation between Lam and a U.K. manager with a particularly dry sense of humor, the latter jokingly commented, "Things will be different when I'm running the company." This comment was made shortly after the acquisition, and so Lam was not familiar with this manager's way of expressing himself, nor was he familiar in general with the slightly sarcastic British sense of humor, which frequently baffles even many native speakers of English who were born and brought up in the United States.

This was not just a problem for Lam. Others in the Dallas office occasionally misinterpreted the humorous intent embedded in communications from their British counterparts, especially when the humor came in e-mail messages. The unthinking use of colloquialisms and slang only added to the problem. This is, perhaps, what playwright George Bernard Shaw meant when he described the United States and England as "two nations divided by a common language."

Conclusion

Despite these new challenges, Radica is doing well and has learned a great deal from the earlier experiences with the Bass Fishin' game project and from the company's more recent experience with the controller projects. In these projects, Radica has had to deal with a number of challenges: building a culture of mutual respect, establishing social norms to reinforce this culture, coordinating tasks across different sites and time zones, communicating and resolving conflicts across different cultures, and making the best use of diverse and widely dispersed competencies, to mention just a few. In the next chapter we will discuss in more detail how Radica dealt with these challenges, and we will identify action steps that may help other organizations deal with the complexities of collaboration across time, distance, and cultures.

Chapter Four

What the Radica Projects Tell Us About Collaboration Across Time, Distance, and Culture

The Radica projects were very different from the John Deere projects, involving just one company collaborating across international boundaries to develop new products that could make or break the company. Despite these differences, many of the same action steps emerged from the Radica case, although with some additional wrinkles. A number of new action steps also came out of this case, particularly those dealing with the special challenges of international and cross-cultural collaboration under intense pressures of time and performance. All the action steps for this case are summarized in Table 4.1.

Phase I: Setting the Stage

The actions that were most instrumental in setting the stage for future collaborations at Radica were those taken by Bob Davids in his work with S. W. Lam in the early years of the company. As they painstakingly constructed the culture, brick by brick, they built the foundation that supports Radica's complex collaborations even to this day.

Build a Culture of Action on a Foundation of Mutual Respect

Radica's culture is made up of two very different dimensions: a pervasive sense of mutual respect and trust, and an uncompromising focus on getting the product out the door. These two aspects may

Table 4.1. Action Steps from the Radica Case

Phase	Action Step
Phase I: Setting the Stage	*Build a culture of action on a foundation of mutual respect*, using norm- and culture-building behavior through public statements, coaching, and consistent actions *Develop lateral skills for collaborating across cultures*, using lateral career moves

Phase II: Getting Started with Specific Projects	*Gain top management's support*
	  Top management actively and visibly supports projects
	  Top management provides access to resources
	
	Put the right people in the right place
	  Create liaison roles
	  Fill liaison roles with people who have good lateral skills
	
	Create collaborative pairs when more than one liaison is involved
	  Use face-to-face interaction to build relationships within pairs
	  Create pairs at management level(s) as well, to provide oversight, escalation paths for resolving conflicts, and so on

Phase III:
Creating the Infrastructure

Lead by facilitating, but exercise authority when necessary, and use clear and unambiguous
   decision-making structures
Structure tasks, by defining, partitioning, and allocating
Rely on communication systems to pull the pieces together

Phase IV:
Doing the Work

Be mindful when communicating
   Be aware of e-mail limitations, and compensate for them with greater attention
   Do not rely exclusively on e-mail
   Instill communication norms by promoting, modeling, and coaching
Use time-zone differences to drive a twenty-four-hour work cycle
Build relationships through travel and face-to-face interaction

Learn from doing

seem incompatible at first glance, but upon closer examination it is clear that they form a dynamic balance, a yin and yang, that has enabled Radica to develop and grow year after year.

The core of Radica's culture reflects Bob's values and his relationship with Lam during the early years in Hong Kong. Bob's attitudes were very different from those of most other Westerners in Hong Kong in those days. He had a more egalitarian attitude and was not condescending or patronizing toward the Chinese workers. Lam had similar values concerning the workers. In Bob's words, they both put themselves "below the workers" and had great respect for them. Bob credited Robert Townsend, a former CEO of Avis and a best-selling business author (see Townsend, 1970, 1984), as a major influence on his leadership philosophy. (Townsend was also a long-term colleague and friend of Bob and joined Radica's board of directors in 1994, at Bob's urging.) Bob cites one Townsend commandment in particular, "Treat people with respect," as the inspiration behind his early efforts at Radica.

Mutual respect was the essence of this culture. Although the term "mutual respect" is widely and often carelessly used, at Radica it had a specific meaning that was clearly linked to identifiable behaviors. It meant that all individuals and groups respected each other's expertise, input, and boundaries. Everyone knew that it was all right to push back and offer dissenting views, another important element of the Radica culture, and everyone also understood that these views had to be taken seriously. In addition, everyone knew when to stop, and when to trust the experience and expertise of others and accept their well-considered judgments.

This mutual respect was particularly evident in the design process for the Bass Fishin' game, involving the product designers in Dallas and the engineers in Hong Kong. This was not the typical "over the wall" development process, dominated and driven by the product designers. Both sides felt free to come up with ideas for the other, and all contributions were equally valued. For example, when Hong Kong made it clear to Dallas, after thoughtful consideration and respectful back-and-forth discussion, that, despite the engineers' best efforts, they just could not include a particular game feature without exceeding the product's price point, Dallas knew that was it. The designers in Dallas trusted the judgment and knowledge of the Hong Kong engineers, and they knew that the engineers' resistance was not arbitrary and capricious. Mutual respect guided all interactions at Radica, between people as well as between sites.

This foundation of goodwill and mutual respect made it possible to sustain the kind of hard-driving momentum needed to succeed in the industry without tearing the company apart. In the toy and game industry, the product has to ship on a certain date—for an annual toy and game show, for example, or for the Christmas shopping season. As Radica's CEO, Pat Feely, notes, "Christmas only comes once a year. If you don't make Christmas, you're doomed." Therefore, the highest priority is to keep things constantly moving forward. Radica cannot afford to stop the process while decisions are pondered or conflicts resolved. "The only way you can stop the process," according to Feely, "is for someone to derail the freight train," and only extraordinary circumstances can do that. The bias is toward action, for keeping things moving, even if that means that mistakes may be made. "People have to keep working even if they may be wrong and it means that someone may critique [their work] later," says Feely. "I think that in the environment we have at Radica, if someone has to make a quick decision in order to keep things on schedule, they won't be criticized for making that decision, even if it ends up being wrong."

To survive in the super-heated, highly competitive, time-critical toy and game industry, Radica has always had to place a premium on performance, but the acquisition of LMP turned the heat up even higher. The acquisition changed Radica from a small, informal company with a familial atmosphere and a strong emphasis on personal relations to a larger, more complex organization that was increasingly reliant on systematic, information-driven processes. It wasn't easy to develop these more formal processes or the cultural context required to support and reinforce them. The changes left more than a few bruises. For some, Radica became a less comfortable place to work. Not surprisingly, the new culture and processes took time to implement, accounting at least in part for the protracted battle over the logo that was described in the previous chapter.

Despite this new focus on formal, systematic processes and "getting product out the door," Radica has tried to hold on to the other side of the company's cultural coin: the "people" dimension. Radica's enduring commitment to mutual respect is what makes all of this work. Mutual respect is reflected as much in personal relationships as in the fairness, objectivity, and openness of the company's processes and policies. The new Radica may seem less like a family than the old Radica, especially to long-term employees, but the company is better prepared to meet the challenges of global competition. The bottom line is that Radica balances its intense focus on timely action and performance by relying on objective processes, trusting in everyone's best intentions and efforts, and tolerating the mistakes that inevitably go hand in hand with a strong bias toward action. Pat Feely sums up the result of this balance in his final word on the logo wars and their aftermath: "I look back at it and see that things went pretty well. The work got done, they still talk to each other, and they still get along."

How did Radica build this culture? It is one thing to talk about a desired culture and something else to actually create it. Culture doesn't just happen. It emerges from people's actions and behavior. Initially it was Bob and Lam, in their interactions with each other and with others at Radica, who built the culture of the organization in its earliest years. In more recent years, Pat Feely and his executive team have further shaped the culture by emphasizing the importance of time-critical performance.

For example, according to Bob, "You don't get angry with your own people. Responses shouldn't be personal, and never cast blame." He established and reinforced these norms by combining public "cheerleading" with one-to-one conversations in which he essentially coached people on their behavior. This was an ongoing process for both Bob and Lam. Since the period of the initial problems associated with the acquisition of LMP, Pat Feely and others on the senior management team have also worked hard to create an environment where disputes are not personalized, win-lose attitudes are not tolerated, and competition and turf battles are rare among employees from different divisions. In addition, they do not let conflicts fester. When serious disagreements come up, they get everybody together, usually on a conference call, to sort out the issues and try to understand one another's positions and concerns.

They have also focused on reducing competition and turf battles between different units, and on making sure that conflicts do not keep products from getting out the door. Like Bob and Lam, Feely and his team do this with public statements and actions that are consistent with the desired culture, and personal feedback and coaching for those whose behavior occasionally deviates from accepted norms. For example, savvy individuals sometimes intentionally wait until the last moment to submit something for approval, knowing that it is likely to be approved because "the freight train cannot be derailed." They get their approval, but they also get timely feedback about their "gaming" the process. Radica's management has also not been shy about encouraging repeat offenders to leave the organization.

Develop Lateral Skills for Collaborating Across Cultures

As we argued in Chapter Two, lateral skills play a very important role in collaborations that successfully cross functional, organizational, and cultural boundaries. Bob Davids demonstrated just how important these skills are in his dealings with the employees in Hong Kong and southern China and in the kinds of values he instilled throughout the company in his years as CEO. Bob saw the same potential in Lam, recognizing early on that Lam had "one foot in each culture." He also realized how critical these skills would be for Radica's future, and so he developed Lam's lateral skills even further by moving him laterally—that is, by sending him to the United States "to teach Americans how to save money," and by having him travel back to Hong Kong, as necessary, "to teach Chinese the American culture and how to work in teams." These lateral skills came in handy when Bob bet Radica's future on an idea for a new game that would eventually transform the nature and the fortunes of the company.

Lateral skills are highly valued in the new Radica as well. This is apparent not so much in what Radica says about the kinds of people the company wants as in the kinds of people the company clearly does not want. "We don't like turf people," notes Pat Feely. "We try to select top management staff that are not driven by silos and power but are driven by teamwork." Jeanne Olsen in the United States and her U.K. counterpart, John Doughty, offer good examples of this essential quality.

Phase II: Getting Started with Specific Projects

The Radica projects reinforce the action steps that emerged from the John Deere case—the importance of gaining top management support, putting the right people in liaison roles, and linking them in collaborative pairs. However, this case reveals another, simpler approach to liaison roles that may work under very special circumstances and conditions.

Gain Top Management's Support

Both Radica projects examined in Chapter Three were top-down projects; that is, they were initiated by Radica's senior management, as are many new product development efforts in other businesses around the world. As top-down projects, they also had considerable high-level support and access to resources, from beginning to end. In fact, the Bass Fishin' game project would not have come about without Bob's support and direct involvement.

Put the Right People in the Right Place

As in the John Deere case, the Bass Fishin' game project and the controller projects also benefited from having skilled people in key liaison roles. What this meant differed significantly, however, from one project to the other. In the Bass Fishin' game project, Lam was the right person, and he filled this role pretty much on his own. His role was pivotal. Without him, the project as well as the company might have failed.

In this project, Lam played a critically important linking role between the design team in Dallas and the engineering team in Hong Kong. He had the responsibility, among others, to alert the designers when features they wanted to include could not be engineered within the price point set for the product or produced with the equipment that was available in the factory in China.

At times Lam also switched hats and played the other side of this linking role, by representing the designers' point of view in his frequent phone conversations with the engineers and on his occasional trips to Hong Kong. It is important to note that Lam played this role in at least three dimensions—linking the designers and the engineers, spanning the cultural differences between the United States and Asia, and interpreting across language differences when necessary. He would not have been able to fulfill these challenging roles without the lateral skills he had developed while growing up in the multicultural mix of Hong Kong, and in his early years at Radica.

Create Collaborative Pairs

The controller projects required a very different approach to linking separate sites. Initially, there were no formally designated liaison roles linking the design teams in Dallas and the United Kingdom. That may have been one of the reasons why the logo wars lasted as long as they did. Once Jeanne Olsen and John Doughty became involved, the war quickly ended. To use the expression we introduced in Chapter Two, they formed a "collaborative pair," in much the same way that Joan and Beverly, Joan and Derek, and "Dr. Deere" and Dave did in the John Deere case. In the case of Jeanne Olsen and John Doughty, however, the collaborative pairing occurred at the executive level. As such, this relationship paved the way for resolution of the conflict. Jeanne and John brought together, in a face-to-face meeting, the two designers who were the principal combatants in the logo wars. In effect, they created a collaborative pairing between the two designers, and their conflict was soon resolved. In Jeanne's words, "Solutions work out much better if you have a relationship with the person you are dealing with." Proactively creating these relationships is the key to avoiding or at least mitigating later problems. It's also important to take note of the critical role of face-to-face contact in creating these relationships. Without that personal contact between the two designers, the logo wars might have lasted even longer than they did.

From the above, we can see that the controller projects required a different approach to liaison roles than the approach used in the earlier, less complicated Bass Fishin' game project. Specifically, Jeanne and John played a similar role, as a pair, that Lam was able to play on his own in the Bass Fishin' game project. It is worth speculating on why one person was able to fulfill the linking role in the Bass Fishin' game project, whereas collaborative pairs were needed in the controller projects, as they also were in the John Deere projects. We suspect that the difference can be attributed to what can be called "organizational separation." Despite the cultural, functional, and geographical distance between the Dallas and Hong Kong sites in the Bass Fishin' game project, there was more that bound the two sites together than pulled them apart. The designers in Dallas and the engineers in Hong Kong all belonged to the same company, and they had all been with Radica for some time when the project was initiated. In addition, they had some common history as separate but linked units—and they had Lam. In other words, the two sites had enough in common to enable someone like

Lam, who had a figurative foot in both sites and well-developed lateral skills, to serve as a highly credible liaison.

In the controller projects, which involved highly distinct units, as in the John Deere case, which involved completely separate organizations, the situation was quite different. If someone like Lam had been available, someone who had a foot in each culture, then a single liaison role might have been enough. But that was not the situation in either case, and there was no other choice than to use different representatives for the different units and organizations. Apparently, that strategy was successful in both cases.

Phase III: Creating the Infrastructure

As already noted, the Radica case is very different from the John Deere case. Nowhere are these differences more apparent than in the actions taken to lay the groundwork for each project. These differences can be seen in how the projects were managed and led, how they were structured, and how Radica dealt with the challenges of international and cross-cultural communication.

Lead by Facilitating, but Exercise Authority When Necessary

Both projects illustrate two very important pieces of our action framework that—on the surface, at least—might appear mutually contradictory: a flexible, facilitative, and adaptable approach to leadership coupled with clear and unambiguous authority. The Bass Fishin' game project is especially instructive in this regard. One of the most striking things about the project was the extent to which leadership was shared among Bob, Lam, and Kevin Brase. As noted in the last chapter Bob was the subject-matter expert; he defined the task and facilitated many of the meetings. Lam provided different perspectives and served as the link between the different functions and cultures in Dallas and Hong Kong. Kevin supervised the designers and managed the project. Among these three, all the key roles and tasks were covered. This shared approach enabled them to match specific leadership competencies with specific tasks.

Bob was clearly the boss, however, and yet he exercised his authority carefully, judiciously, and only when necessary. His skill in facilitating the team played a particularly important role in the project's success. His facilitation reflected the values of mutual trust and respect that he and Lam had worked so hard to instill into Radica's culture. As a result, discussions were open, freewheeling, and sometimes heated. Some tension was created, of course, but the unspoken rule, which Bob was quick to reinforce when he had to, was that voices were never raised, regardless of differences. Bob also made sure that differences were never personalized and that unpopular positions were not held against the people expressing them. As necessary, however—for example, if the team was stymied and could not reach a decision on its own—Bob stepped in and made decisions. Once a decision was made, everybody was prepared to accept it, whether it had been made by the group or by Bob, and move on to the next task.

Lam sums up this approach by drawing on his interest in military strategy: "Bob wants to get as many of his troops involved in the decision as possible, but he is the boss." Lam was the one most likely to voice dissenting opinions, but when Bob needed to step in and make a decision, Lam was like a good soldier and was one of the first to get in line behind his leader and follow his orders, regardless of any lingering reservations he might still have.

The situation was more complex for the controller projects. The company at that point was larger and more dispersed, and authority was necessarily more diffuse and less personal. No single person could have overseen everything and intervened every time a difficult decision had to be made. This was particularly apparent with respect to the problems that emerged between the U.S. and U.K. designers. By contrast with the Bass Fishin' game project, tasks in the controller projects could not be cleanly separated between the U.S. and U.K. teams; the team members were all designers, and they were all working on the same project. The initial conflicts re-sulted from the teams' interdependence as well as from the absence of the kind of face-to-face relationship building that would have developed naturally if the designers had been able to work side by side on the same tasks. They tried developing the product jointly and virtually, but that approach just didn't work, as the logo wars so dramatically demonstrated.

They eventually resolved the conflict and learned a valuable lesson in the process. As Pat Feely says, "Someone has to be ulti-mately responsible. Lines of authority have to be clearly drawn. We have to be very clear about who is responsible for what." Now there are clear lines of authority as well as clear escalation paths for push-ing decisions up the management hierarchy for resolution when controversies and differences get especially heated. In addition, the company's bias toward action keeps things moving forward while issues, differences, and conflicts are addressed. Someone always has clearly designated authority and can step in quickly to make deci-sions when time is running out and conflicts threaten to create seri-ous delays in getting the product out the door. Radica might have been able to avoid much of the conflict and delay that plagued the controller projects if such an unambiguous authority structure had been in place before the project began.

Clear authority is an easy dimension to overlook when the fo-cus is on images of the lively give-and-take of collaborative inter-actions, but it is just as important to successful collaboration as is the more familiar focus on leveling authority that is implied by such concepts as mutual respect and empowerment. The meshing of authority and participation, of hierarchy and flexibility, so aptly illustrated by the Radica case is, in our opinion, the key to collabo-rative leadership. Effective collaboration requires decisive leaders—leaders who not only facilitate open, honest, and frank discussion among everyone involved but who are also willing to make deci-sions and resolve conflicts when the need arises. At first glance, these features may seem mutually exclusive, but in the context of the kind of complex collaborations described in this book, they are clearly complementary. Leaders need to learn how to walk the fine line between authority and participation. This relationship between the two parallels the relationship discussed at the beginning of this chapter: between the bias toward action, on the one hand, and goodwill and mutual trust, on the other. This issue offers yet another illustration of the intrinsic connection between the dimensions of structure and relationship in complex collaborations across multiple boundaries.

Structure Tasks

Radica has been a geographically, culturally, and functionally complex organization ever since the company established its Dallas office, in the early 1990s. During the Bass Fishin' game project, the company dealt with this complexity in a number of ways. One of the most important means used for collaborating across the potential barriers of time, distance and culture was organizing and structuring Radica's new product development process to take advantage of the diverse competencies that can be found in global organizations like Radica where "the sun never sets." But the company also had to compensate for the considerable cultural and geographical complexities created by the company's increasingly dispersed "footprint." How the company accomplished this task suggests a number of action steps that other organizations, facing similar challenges, might undertake early in their projects to lay the foundation for their work.

A very important step in Radica's successful approach to complex collaboration was defining and partitioning the various tasks—product design, engineering, and manufacturing—that were involved in the development process and allocating those tasks to teams of people who had the appropriate expertise. The members of each separate team had to be "co-located"—that is, they had to be in the same physical location at the same time. Design work, for example, requires creativity and intense short-cycle back-and-forth interactions among all the people involved. It is a task best accomplished in real time, and on a face-to-face basis, even when advanced collaboration technology is available. In other words, the members of Radica's design team were "reciprocally interdependent"—they all needed to work closely with other team members to get their work done. The same could be said about the engineering team in Hong Kong: engineering work also requires creativity, involves tasks that are reciprocally interdependent, and is best accomplished when most members of the team are co-located.

On the other hand, the separate teams were not as dependent on each other as were the members within each team. The product designers did need the engineers to transform their ideas into actual game features, and the engineers did need the designers' ideas before they could do their work, but the interactions between the design and engineering teams were not as intense as they were within each of the teams and did not have to be synchronized as closely. Therefore, if the tasks could be defined and designed appropriately, the two teams did not need to be co-located. They could be located where the relative competencies were abundant and available at relatively low cost. That is why Bob decided to co-locate all the product designers in Dallas, and the engineers in Hong Kong. There were also other reasons, of course—for example, Radica already had a sales and distribution group in Dallas, and Bob wanted design to be "close to the market"—but defining, partitioning, and allocating the tasks as Bob did were no doubt some of the most important steps in the project's success.

Not all critical interdependencies between the two sites could be eliminated, however, nor should they have been eliminated even if it had been possible to do so. The designers and engineers needed to work together to create a product that could be built, would function effectively and could be sold at a cost that would yield a profit. Therefore, the decision to partition the two teams' functions carefully and allocate each piece of the work to the appropriate location would only work if Radica could create some means of pulling the separate pieces back together again. The challenge became how to integrate these two essential functions, design and engineering, given the geographical and cultural distances between them.

Rely on Communication Systems to Pull the Pieces Together

Radica relied on a number of means, both in the Bass Fishin' game project and in the controller projects, to bring about this integration. The company's shared culture of mutual trust was one such means. Also helpful was the fact that the same values and norms that went along with mutual trust tended to promote open, respectful communication across the cultural and functional differences at each site. The linking of roles was another such means (for example, Lam's role as a liaison between Hong Kong and Dallas, and the collaborative pairing that took place between Jeanne Olsen in the United States and John Doughty in the United Kingdom).

Yet another means—another type of "glue"—was communication. Radica used a lot of this glue and has continued to do so over the years, employing a variety of ways to communicate across geographical and cultural divides. In the days of the Bass Fishin' game project, it was mostly fax technology and express shipping, supplemented by the occasional telephone call and the even more occasional trip, that linked the different teams collaborating on the project. More sophisticated high-tech communications media—e-mail, videoconferencing, and 3-D design software—had been added to the mix by the time the controller projects began. But it wasn't the technology alone that tied the different sites together.

The technology made communication possible, of course, but it was shared norms, expectations, and understandings about how best to use it that enabled the company to move beyond basic communication to creative collaboration. These norms developed as Radica used the new technologies and wrestled with the new challenges they presented, challenges that were increasingly evident as the company dived more deeply into its primary tasks. The way

Radica overcame these challenges produced the norms and expectations that turned out to be the strongest glue of all.

Phase IV: Doing the Work

The problems of collaboration across great distances, both geographical and cultural, were especially apparent in Radica's use of e-mail. As many individuals and organizations have learned in recent years, e-mail makes it easier to communicate without thinking, and without the social cues that might otherwise soften the impact of hasty, ill-conceived messages. The Radica teams learned quickly from their early experience with this medium. Their strong foundation of mutual respect and their other, related cultural values enabled them to develop norms, expectations, and behaviors for dealing with the communication challenges of the new Radica. The way they dealt with the complexities of communicating across the four regional cultures involved in the controller projects was essentially the same as in the days before the Bass Fishin' game project—except, of course, that the situation was even more complex.

Be Mindful When Communicating

The Radica teams quickly learned that the best way to deal with the limitations of e-mail was to be aware of them and compensate by paying more attention to what they said and how they said it. Buddhists call this kind of attention the process of being "mindful"; cognitive behavioral therapists refer to it as "metacognition." Whatever it may be called, it means using self-awareness to avoid potentially problematic behavior by catching oneself and modifying the behavior before it leads to trouble. The Radica teams may not have been familiar with either the spiritual concept of mindfulness or the psychotherapeutic concept of metacognition, but they soon "got it" in their own way and incorporated this type of self-awareness into their communication behavior.

They did so by recognizing the possibility of miscommunication and therefore being very careful about how they communicated with team members in different countries. Everyone involved tried to be as direct and to the point as possible in their e-mails. Slang, colloquialisms, and obscure, culturally based references and quips were consciously avoided. The team members were especially careful about cultural differences in humor. They learned to expect the unexpected, and to avoid the seemingly harmless quip that unintentionally offends. Everyone made a concerted effort to take cultural differences into consideration. As a result, they rapidly developed a fair degree of tolerance for and understanding of the occasional well-intentioned but off-putting slip of the tongue or keystroke.

Because they were sensitive to potential language problems, they worked hard to make sure that their communications were understood. They often reworded communications from each other to clarify what was being said. ("Let me put this in my own words to make sure that I understand what you are saying. Tell me if I am not getting it right.") Once they got to know each other, as well as each other's English-language habits, understanding became easier. In other words, given the barriers of language, culture, and distance, they compensated by being extra careful. The U.K. director of design summed it up as follows: "Geographical distance forces attention to communication. Being pleasant and treating people with respect is universal."

Another important lesson was not to rely exclusively on e-mail to clarify and resolve misunderstandings. This lesson is still reflected in current practice. In the words of one interviewee, people "think before they jump;" that is, whenever anyone receives a potentially provocative or insensitive e-mail, he or she picks up the phone and talks directly with the person who sent it, even if that means staying late because of the time difference. Because there is an overlap of two hours between the usual workday in Hong Kong and the U.K. workday, people at those sites have more opportunities to communicate by phone around critical design issues than was true in the earlier project. As one of the Hong Kong engineers has noted, "With e-mail it takes several days of going back and forth before you finally realize that you need to talk directly to resolve the issue."

It is important to note that Radica had to reinforce these norms after acquiring LMP and then had to update them to fit the new context. Before and during the Bass Fishin' game project, Radica worked hard to develop norms that respected the different cultures represented in the company of the time (the early to mid-1990s). The acquisition of LMP unexpectedly changed everything. Radica initially underestimated the cultural impact of the acquisition, assuming that the addition of the U.K. culture did not represent a great change from the existing cultural mix. But the company soon learned otherwise. Furthermore, the new communications technology, e-mail, exacerbated the potential for unintended cultural slights and miscommunication. Once Radica recognized the problem, the company moved quickly to reinforce the earlier values of mutual respect, cultural sensitivity, and mindfulness, recalibrating them for the new technological and business conditions.

This development suggests that other organizations may need to do likewise whenever they add new partners to their complex collaborations. In fact, it is probably a good idea for every organization to assess its culture periodically, regardless of whether it has made any significant acquisitions or changes. The organization should then consciously act to reinforce or even adjust the values and norms that are the foundations of the desired culture. Developing appropriate norms requires more than good intentions, of course. The cultural sensitivity and communications awareness that has marked Radica since its earliest years is not something that just appeared on its own. Radica understood that, even with the best of intentions, it is possible to forget manners and customs, especially those of a culture different from one's own. The company worked hard to internalize rather than memorize these expectations, to make them implicit, tacit, intuitive guides to everyday behavior that did not have to be thought about every moment of the day.

The key to developing and internalizing these norms, of course, was the explicit and consistent behavior of Bob, Lam, Pat Feely, and other members of the management team. Just as they had done in building Radica's culture, they instilled the communication norms that reflected and reinforced the company's culture by publicly promoting these norms, modeling them whenever they could, and coaching others whenever that was necessary.

Use Time-Zone Differences to Drive a Twenty-Four-Hour Work Cycle

In addition to norms of cultural sensitivity, Radica's leaders established an expectation of daily communication among collaborating sites. This expectation was critical in the effort to transform the obstacles of distance and time zones into a twenty-four-hour work cycle. During the Bass Fishin' game project, for example, the Dallas product designers used the daily schedule and the difference in time zones to break their task into segments that they could forward to Hong Kong every day, as described in Chapter Three. The Hong Kong team members would reply with their feedback by the end of their workday, and the Dallas team members responded to the feedback by the end of their own next workday. And so it went. If team members had no immediate feedback or response to a fax from the other team, they still acknowledged receipt of the communication and estimated how long it would take them to send a more substantive reply. Everybody understood that some form of daily communication between sites was necessary and expected.

This norm had its roots in the earliest days of the company. Bob, for example, felt that "everybody deserved a response every day, even if the response was 'we are working on it; we will get back to you in a week.'" Not surprisingly, Lam had a similar view, believing that the basis of communication is response: "People need to reply to messages." The Bass Fishin' game project teams were small, and under Lam's direct supervision, so he was able to manage the communication process and provide personal feedback and coaching to team members at each site, to ensure prompt responses to faxes from their collaborators overseas.

Even with newer technologies and newer projects, Radica's twenty-four-hour work cycle has not changed. It was a critical factor in the success of the controller projects and is very much a part of Radica today. When Pat Feely gets to work in the morning, he has e-mail from the United Kingdom, and by the end of the day he is getting e-mail from Hong Kong, too. The bottom line, as Kevin Brase notes, is that people at Radica "work hard to maintain a constant flow of communication."

Build Relationships Through Travel and Face-to-Face Interaction

Even with all of the new communications technology, Radica still sees the need to travel among the various sites that make up the company's far-flung "empire." Videoconferencing, which would seem to offer many of the advantages of face-to-face (FTF) interaction without the cost and inconvenience, has not been an adequate substitute. From Pat Feely's perspective, "Videoconferencing is about 30 percent better than phone—enough to be worth the cost of the equipment and the long-distance charges, but not enough to replace FTF interaction." Therefore, people at Radica travel more to meet face to face with their counterparts, especially if the issues are critical and difficult. These meetings can produce the kind of intensely focused attention needed to keep conflicts from boiling over. Travel serves another purpose as well. According to the U.K. design director, "The only way to do design is to see it with your own eyes, to see the physical constraints, the issues that the people you are working with at a distance have to deal with."

Travel and face-to-face meetings can be used more proactively as well, to build relationships that can help prevent problems or make it easier to deal with problems when they do occur. In the early days of the controller projects, Radica's approach was more reactive, as demonstrated by the controversy over the logo. Problem solving was ad hoc and done on the fly as time-critical issues came up. A number of our interviewees felt that the start of the two projects might have gone more smoothly if more travel for face-to-face meetings had been built in at the beginning, before conflicts emerged.

Radica now recognizes the importance of moving people around to meet and get to know their counterparts at different sites and learn about their culture. Senior management is especially sensitive to this issue. The U.K. division head, John Doughty, talks about the importance of "swapping people" among the United Kingdom, the United States, and Hong Kong, saying that this practice "leads to better understanding of the subtleties of each other's culture. That makes it easier to bite your tongue before making the sarcastic comment." His counterpart, Jeanne Olsen, says, "If you have the opportunity to spend some time with" a colleague at another site, it is "easier to work out issues via e-mail or phone. Once you know who the person is, what their motivations are, they are not just a name on an e-mail." With respect to the conflict over the logo, she concludes, "We would have solved it much faster if we could have gotten all of the key people together in the same room and had these meetings beforehand." She sums this up well in her final word on the subject: "Before I had an issue, I had a relationship."

Radica also sees travel and face-to-face contact as useful for employees at lower levels, where the opportunities for developing relationships with potential collaborators are not as great. Creating relationships at these operational levels is especially important because these employees tend to be younger, less mature, and therefore more likely than those at higher levels of the organization to be competitive, to be ego-involved, and to take things personally. As a result, Radica management has expanded the function of the company's quarterly ideation meetings to get "designers from both sides of the pond together," to use John Doughty's words, who are jointly working on issues critical to current projects. Even that may not be enough, in the eyes of one interviewee: "It would be great if we could meet face to face more often. We have more need for that now. We are bigger, and there are more projects. The projects themselves are more complex—there are more approvals and reviews and more people are involved. The bottom line is that there are now more opportunities for miscommunication and conflict."

Learn from Doing

Many of the action steps described in the preceding several pages were taken in reaction to problems that emerged in the course of the projects' work. That is, project team members learned to be mindful in their communications because they had noticed problems as they did their work, and they addressed these problems by modifying their communication behavior. This illustrates the importance of informal learning processes, which involve casual observations about what works and what does not, individual modifications of behavior to improve task performance and work processes, and informal sharing with co-workers of what has been learned.

Recognizing the value of these informal learning processes, Radica management decided to go a step farther by formally capturing, documenting, integrating, and disseminating these learnings across the company. In other words, the company decided to transform its largely informal learning processes into something more systematic and potentially more powerful. The primary arena for this formal learning process is a semiannual face-to-face meeting involving the management of the groups involved in Radica's collaborative processes (product development, manufacturing, and finance). The venue for the meeting usually alternates between Hong Kong and Dallas. Participants use the meeting to discuss their work processes for the purpose of identifying and addressing problems and improving the processes in general. Everyone contributes to the agenda, and minutes are distributed after the meeting to identify follow-up tasks and due dates. Different projects and different conditions may require different processes, but the bottom line is the same: it is important to monitor processes and outcomes, reflect on and learn from the information that is generated, and adapt and modify tasks, behavior, plans, and even goals.

Conclusion

A comparison between Tables 2.1 and 4.1 shows that the two cases presented so far have much in common, despite considerable differences between them. Many of the action steps suggested by the two cases, especially the steps common to both, illustrate the dynamic and intrinsic connection between relationships and structure in collaborations that cross multiple boundaries. In particular, the creation of liaison roles, essentially a structural intervention, will have little positive impact in and of itself unless people with good lateral skills are assigned to fill these roles. Further, the right people in those roles, linked by strong working relationships, can create the structure needed to guide and focus their own collaborations as well as those between the teams and organizations that they represent.

Our next and final case, presented in the following chapter, has similarities to the John Deere and Radica cases. Like the John Deere case, it features collaborations among different organizations. Like the Radica case, it entails collaborations that are critical to the immediate success of all the organizations involved. There is also a significant cross-cultural/international dimension to these collaborations. In effect, the next case has it all; and, despite what it has in common with the first two cases, it is more than the sum of those two. It is clearly the most complex of the three, a supply-chain collaboration reaching across great distance, different organizations, and diverse cultures. More than either of the first two previous cases, it truly represents a business without boundaries.

Chapter Five

Across the Supply Chain

The Solectron Case

In the fall of 2002, a labor dispute shut down ports up and down the West Coast of the United States. Ships loaded with supplies sat idle at the docks or at anchor in the waters outside the ports. For several days, factories around the world could not ship their materials, parts, and products; factories in North America could not get the supplies they needed to assemble final products; distributors and stores had fewer products to sell to their customers. The global economy was in danger of grinding to a halt. The economic threat was so great that after only a few days President George W. Bush invoked the rarely used Taft-Hartley Act to order the ports to open and the workers to report back to their jobs.

This incident demonstrates not only how tightly linked organizations are around the world but also how important these linkages are to the health and vitality of the global economy. Supply chains—the highly interdependent flow of parts, subassemblies, and final products from suppliers through manufacturers to customers—are the mechanisms by which far-flung webs of organizations put goods into the hands of consumers around the world. Each link in these chains must not only accomplish these tasks at low cost and with high quality but must also do it "just in time." There is little margin for error in this world. The winners are those organizations that can master the intricate timing and global choreography required by this vast goods-producing machinery.

The case we examine in this chapter concerns the complex collaborations that are the building blocks of these global supply chains. We focus here on one of the big winners in this highly competitive, rapidly changing industry. Solectron Corporation has been a pioneer and a leader in this industry since the company's inception, in 1977. Solectron started out as a contract manufacturer, handling the manufacturing overflow from such original equipment manufacturers (OEMs) as Hewlett-Packard, IBM, and Sony. Solectron was well positioned to take advantage of the outsourcing boom of the 1980s by providing world-class manufacturing capabilities to companies that wanted to focus on their own core competencies, particularly on product development and marketing. In the 1990s Solectron twice won the Malcolm Baldrige Award for quality in manufacturing, the first company to do so in the history of the award.

The industry continues to change, reflecting the dynamic economic, geopolitical, and technological environment in which it operates. Solectron continues to innovate and shape this increasingly important and challenging industry, having evolved from its relatively modest roots as a contract manufacturer for the computer and consumer electronics industry to what the company and others now describe as a global supply-chain facilitator—that is, a company that can manage the entire supply chain, in Solectron's words, "across the entire product life cycle." Solectron now handles "all the actions, processes, and relationships necessary to turn a great idea into a great product—and to keep it in great working condition for the end-user . . . from the time a product is conceived all the way through repair and end of life" (Solectron Corporation, 2002, p. 6).

Examining supply-chain collaborations from the point of view of the supply-chain facilitator is especially useful for understanding what helps make these complex collaborations work. Solectron's position in the middle of the supply chain, between customers and suppliers, enables us to look both up and down the supply chain. Furthermore, Solectron's emerging role as a facilitator of the entire supply chain provides the big picture. All of this gives us a unique perspective on the complex collaborations among all the parties that make up this increasingly important industry.

As in the case examined in Chapter Two, this one involves an interorganizational collaboration, but with some very important differences. For our purposes, the most important difference is that supply chains feature tightly linked, highly interdependent, time-critical interactions that are central to the core work of the participating organizations. The interactions involved in the John Deere case (Chapter Two) were not chainlike—that is, tightly linked and highly interdependent—because most of the time the key organizations did not have to work very closely, unlike typical supply-chain collaborators. Nor was the task described in the earlier case—the development of a college-based training program—central to the primary work of the key organizations. Therefore, the case presented in this chapter and the next enables us to examine interorganizational collaborations that are deeper and more intimate, and where the organizations involved have much more to gain or lose from the outcomes. In the case examined here, the success of the organizations involved depended on the complex collaborations that inextricably tied them together.

About Solectron

Over the years, a number of factors have shaped the complex collaborations that collectively comprise the business of supply-chain manufacturing. Not surprisingly, the ebb and flow of the economy is one of the most important. No other industry has been as vulnerable to fluctuations in the business cycle than contract manufacturing, especially in the electronics manufacturing services (EMS) industry. When the economy is booming, contract manufacturing booms along with it, and when the economy goes bust . . . well, you get the picture. The industry hasn't been around very long, and so the companies have not experienced as many ups and downs as, say, the automobile industry, but the rapidity and amplitude of the swings makes this business as volatile as they come.

The 1990s were especially volatile. After a period of prolonged sluggishness in the early years of the decade, the EMS industry feasted along with almost everyone else during the dot-com boom in the latter part of the decade. This era fostered tremendous growth in the industry, and, like many other companies, Solectron went on a buying spree, acquiring factories and other electronics and computer-related companies around the globe. The factories Solectron acquired helped the company deal with the surge in demand for its manufacturing services, fueled by the overheated growth in technology-related industries. Then the dot-com bust put the brakes on the economy as a whole, and on the technology industries in particular. EMS companies, which are right in the middle of the push-and-pull of supply and demand, were hit especially hard. Solectron suffered along with the rest, going from $18 billion in sales revenue in FY01 to about $12 billion the following year. As this case was being written, the first signs that the economy might be coming out of the post "dot-bomb" doldrums were beginning to emerge, and it was expected that signs of a similar recovery in Solectron's fortunes would not be far behind.

The reason this is so important is the impact that these business fluctuations have on Solectron's relationships with its customers and suppliers, relationships that are at the core of the complex collaborations among all of them. In a nutshell, when times are good, demand is strong, and supplies can run short. The success of OEMs and EMS companies alike depends on reliable suppliers—that is, those companies that can deliver an uninterrupted stream of reliable, low-cost parts. Just the opposite is true when business is slow. In those conditions, the OEMs and the EMS companies are in the driver's seat, and suppliers do everything they can to court their favor and thus ensure a steady market for their products.

Relationships can get strained in these changing conditions, and good relationships among all three parties—OEMs, EMS companies, and suppliers—are necessary to carry them through uncertain times. For example, during an economic slowdown, when demand is slow, Solectron needs to exercise restraint and not try to squeeze every last penny from the price of a part provided by a preferred supplier because Solectron may have to count on the same supplier for a continuous stream of parts when demand picks up again. The impact of changing economic conditions on supply-chain relationships was dramatically illustrated by the economic slowdown at the beginning of this decade. Consumer demand slowed precipitously with many orders and parts already in the pipeline. In the words of Eddie Maxey, vice president of global supply management, "It was like somebody turned out the lights." In these circumstances, somebody has to "eat the excess"—that is, absorb the cost of parts, supplies, and subassemblies that are no longer needed. This situation can have significant bottom-line implications for all the companies involved. Not surprisingly, this situation can strain relationships among collaborators if it is not handled fairly, professionally, and as amicably as possible.

Solectron's relationships with its customers roughly mirror the company's relationships with its suppliers, with Solectron serving, in effect, as a supplier to the OEMs with which it works. Therefore, the tensions are similar, but with Solectron in a role that is the reverse image of the one just described. Solectron would like to create some stability in this stressful, turbulent environment and control or at least mitigate the impact of the economic fluctuations that have whipsawed the company back and forth since its earliest days. Therefore, Solectron's goal is to transcend the volatility and transform the adversity by creating relationships that can ensure steady business, low costs, and uninterrupted production.

To make matters even more complex, many of these new relationships span international boundaries. For many businesses, globalization means moving manufacturing from one geographical region to another, in a constant search for ever-lower labor and material costs. This has been especially true for the EMS industry, Solectron included. That is why most of Solectron's acquisitions in the late 1990s were in Asia (for example, in Malaysia, Singapore, and China), with the company taking over many of the plants divested by OEMs like Nortel, Ericsson, IBM, and Texas Instruments, which were increasingly outsourcing their manufacturing to companies like Solectron. Solectron expects that all its manufacturing within the next few years will be in China, and that even more of the company's supplier base will be located in Asia than is the case now. As a result, not all of Solectron's most critical and challenging relationships are external, that is, with customers and suppliers. Some are internal to the company, especially those involving the geographically dispersed sites that Solectron acquired at the end of the last decade. Integrating these acquisitions—with all the cultural, linguistic, and geopolitical challenges they pose—has been a top priority for the last several years.

To summarize, OEMs, supply-chain facilitators like Solectron, and suppliers need to collaborate closely to ensure a steady flow of orders, products, and parts. These collaborative relationships are constantly being tested by fluctuating economic conditions, cultural boundaries, and the unrelenting imperative for improved performance. The links both among and within supply-chain partners are becoming increasingly critical, complex, and difficult. Therefore, the key challenge for all the organizations involved in today's global supply chains is to develop, maintain, strengthen, and leverage the relationships that drive performance. How has Solectron dealt with these critically important issues over the last several years? Given the company's role as a pioneer in this dynamic industry, what Solectron is doing in the face of these challenges can tell us a lot about complex collaborations in the new global economy.

Building Supplier Relationships Through Information, Performance, and Formal Structure

Solectron's strategy for building new kinds of relationships with its supply-chain collaborators can be seen in how the company works with its suppliers. These new relationships are now based on a foundation of performance metrics, information, and formal contracts. Paul DeMand, vice president of electromechanical systems, sees these relationships as more "professional" than they have been in the past. That is, there is less emphasis on personal relationships and "handshakes" and more emphasis on performance as defined by formal contracts and as assessed by comprehensive, reliable, and timely measurement systems.

DeMand characterizes this change in very broad terms as a "switch from relationship-oriented guys chasing parts to engineers chasing performance." In the past, these relationships were informal and personal; building and maintaining them required a great deal of "schmoozing" and "doing lunch." There was little consistency from site to site, and from buyer to buyer. The collaborators' styles, approaches, and relationships varied widely and depended on the personal characteristics of the individual buyers and suppliers' representatives. Agreements were sealed by handshakes and often little else. Things are very different now. Relationships are still important, but they are now based more on performance and contracts than on personalities.

The Supplier Scorecard and the Quarterly Business Review. The primary vehicle for these new, more formal, performance-based relationships is what is known as the supplier scorecard. Every quarter, each of Solectron's one hundred most important, "preferred" suppliers is formally evaluated on a number of metrics, including price, terms and conditions, quality, on-time delivery, technology, support/service, and the like. Solectron refers to this evaluation as the "quarterly business review" (QBR). The scorecard is prepared in advance of the review and is sent to the supplier. Then meetings are held. The location varies; sometimes a meeting takes place at a Solectron plant where problems and issues with particular "commodities" (parts) have been most troublesome. Separate reviews are conducted with each supplier of the part in question. Attendees include the supplier team, the team's counterparts from Solectron, the commodity buyers, and the team managers. Higher-level managers and executives may also attend if problems have been serious enough.

The meetings, which typically run from half a day to a full day, are designed for mutual problem solving rather than for pointing fingers, placing blame, and generally beating up on the suppliers. Frequently a meeting begins with the Solectron reviewers explaining how they came up with the scores they did. The suppliers then have an opportunity to respond to the data. They may dispute the scores and even argue that Solectron is the source of the problem. Others at the plant can be brought into the discussion, to provide further information and help get to the root of the problems. The important point is that the scorecards are used as the takeoff point for discussion; they are not the last word. The scorecard helps to focus discussion on problem diagnosis and solutions to help suppliers improve their performance. The approach is collaborative, involving both Solectron and the supplier teams. The stakes are high in this process: Solectron is more inclined to move business to those suppliers that consistently score well in their QBRs.

The view from the suppliers' perspective is much the same, as can be seen in the following comments from a representative of FCI Electronics, a supplier of connector systems for Solectron:

> The process works pretty well. Solectron is good at telling you whether or not you're doing well. . . . We get the scorecard two weeks in advance and do a worldwide conference call the week before the QBR to discuss the issues that came up in the scorecard. This takes out any surprises, which is important because this can be a very emotional process. . . . Most of the time they are fair reports. They open up lines of communication about their perception of our performance. . . . Solectron is very well prepared for the meetings. They have agendas, and everything is set up before the meetings begin.

The supplier representative does note that Solectron also uses the QBRs to squeeze further price concessions from its suppliers—after all, price is heavily weighted on the scorecards. But it's not always about knocking another penny or two off the cost of a part. Solectron will often pass on an opportunity to get a lower price if the company can count on the supplier to guarantee delivery when demand picks up. Of course, to make the other benefits worthwhile to Solectron, the supplier has to be close enough in price to lower-cost competitors. As this representative notes, "You have to have a good relationship with them to be able to do this. That's where the relationships become important." He agrees with Paul DeMand, however, that relationships between Solectron and its suppliers are "more than just a couple of beers and hot dogs. . . . They have to be based on good business principles." He also notes, in what is appropriately the last word on this issue, that "not everyone uses scorecards, but those that do are more successful."

From Handshakes to Contracts. These principles of good business also include replacing handshakes with contracts, another critical element in Solectron's changing relationships with its suppliers. There is still plenty of handshaking, but informal agreements are more likely now than in the past to be codified in formal contracts. Solectron used to be fairly casual about its agreements with suppliers, but, according to the suppliers, now does a much better job than its competitors of documenting agreements. Solectron documents almost everything, archives all correspondence, and relies on a contract template that typically runs twenty-five pages or more and covers almost everything, from price and delivery date to liabilities, warranties, cancellation policies, and patent agreements.

The contracts have been very helpful in resolving conflicts arising from sudden downturns, cancelled orders, and the issue of who has to "eat" the excess. These issues are now spelled out in the contracts. Like the scorecards and the QBRs, however, the contracts can also be used as the basis for further discussions, which can strengthen relationships in the long run while addressing the issues at hand. As Paul DeMand notes, "Everyday things get negotiated outside the contract. Life is compromise and negotiation. The document is a starting point, but we can be open and flexible, depending on how serious the issue is, of course. We're not screamers. We don't overdemand." DeMand cites the example of an otherwise reliable supplier who made a major mistake by shipping the wrong part, shutting down production as a result. "But this supplier had done extraordinary things for Solectron in the past when we made mistakes. I didn't penalize them for their mistake, even though I could have, according to the contract." In this case, the long-term relationship with a usually reliable supplier was more important than short-term monetary compensation for the mistake. In the future, the shoe may be on the other foot—for example, Solectron may need a rapid, unplanned delivery of critical materials to fulfill a customer order—and the supplier may be in a position to return the favor.

The Supplier Council.   The flow of information and feedback is not just one way, from Solectron to its suppliers. The company offers several vehicles by which suppliers can provide feedback, information, and advice to Solectron. One of the most interesting and valuable is the Supplier Council, which is sponsored by Solectron's materials organization, the division responsible for everything concerning the materials that make up the customer's product. The council is made up of representatives from twelve of Solectron's major suppliers and meets about three times a year. The purpose of the council is to provide the suppliers' perspective on emerging trends and best practices in the electronics industry, to identify specific issues or problems that have come up in doing business with Solectron, and to focus on areas for improvement. The supplier representatives are typically high-level executives who have particular insights into the electronics industry. The companies represented on the council are usually drawn from distinct supplier categories—for example, connectors, printed circuit boards, and the like—and are chosen in such a way that direct competitors are not represented on the council at the same time.

The all-day meetings tend to be animated and frank. A meeting may start with the Solectron representatives, usually senior executives from the materials organization, sharing some confidential information to encourage candid discussion. The council may focus on a couple of issues during the meeting, and then teams are formed to work on these issues after the meeting and to report back at the next meeting. Issues that have been raised and addressed by the Supplier Council include the large number of Solectron people with whom suppliers need to interact in order to get things done, what Solectron can do to make its online purchasing tools easier to use, and how best to bring suppliers into the design of the supply-chain process. The council meetings have been so successful from Solectron's point of view that Kevin Burns, Solectron's chief materials officer at the time of our interviews, considered the Supplier Council to be like an "extended staff" (Carbone, 2003, p. 6).

Standardized Processes and Practices. This new emphasis on performance metrics and contracts has the added benefit of standardizing processes and practices across the many dispersed sites that now comprise the Solectron "footprint." One consequence of Solectron's aggressive acquisitions strategy during the heady days of the new economy was different ways of doing business from one site to another. Processes and practices were often based on the personalities of individual buyers and on the cultures of the sites where they worked, making it very difficult for supplier representatives who had to deal with multiple buyers with different styles and expectations.

Another initiative that helps make suppliers' jobs easier and improves the effectiveness of Solectron's procurement processes is a Web-based procurement tool that was recently implemented at all the company's sites. According to Kevin Burns, this standardized tool "automates the purchasing process, allowing purchase orders, [acknowledgments], order changes and forecasts to be transmitted to suppliers via the Internet" (Carbone, 2003, p. 6). Suppliers, like FCI Electronics, that also use this system to track delivery and provide information about the orders they fill have welcomed the move toward standardized processes and practices by means of the scorecard, the quarterly business reviews, the standardized contracts, and the Web-based purchasing tool. These changes provide some predictability and consistency from site to site and makes it easier for them to focus on what's really important when doing business with

Solectron. Solectron now speaks to them with one voice rather than many.

Building Customer Relationships by Offering Greater Value

Closer relationships with customers is the other side of Solectron's strategy of "deep collaboration" (our expression, not theirs). Again, the mirror-image metaphor applies: just as Solectron's goal is to increase its suppliers' value to Solectron, the company is also trying to increase the value it offers to its customers. Solectron is striving to accomplish this goal by offering a wider range of world-class services and providing up-to-the-minute, comprehensive information that can inform customers' strategies and business decisions as well as the company's own.

Greater Value Through New Services. As described earlier, Solectron has evolved from being a contract manufacturer, handling overflow manufacturing for electronics companies, to acting as a de facto manufacturing division for many of the leading companies within this industry. Most technology companies no longer manufacture their own products, and many of the newer ones never did. Instead, they outsource their manufacturing to companies like Solectron, which can leverage their experience, expertise, and widespread supplier bases to get quality parts at the lowest prices in the most timely fashion and assemble them rapidly, reliably, and efficiently.

Solectron has now moved on to the next stage in this evolutionary process by offering a wider range of services that encompass the entire product life cycle. According to one of the company's recent annual reports, "From the time a product is conceived all the way through repair and end of life, our services, products and solutions make our customers more competitive" (Solectron Corporation, 2002, p. 6). Product design is one of the areas that Solectron is now aggressively marketing as one of the new services that the company can offer to OEMs. In the words of Vincent DePalma, vice president of technology and new product integration,

> Outsourcing product design helps streamline the supply chain process. Involving EMS companies early on ensures a rapid, cost effective transition from product concept to volume manufacturing. . . . EMS providers work with OEMs in the early stages of the design process to develop and implement design guidelines for ease in manufacturing processes and component selection for better cost and availability. . . . Involving EMS providers in design guidelines, layout, component selection, design analysis, sourcing and prototyping results in the greatest probability of success [DePalma, 2002, n.p.].

The nature of these services requires closer collaboration between Solectron and its customers, not just a hand-off of manufacturing requirements from the customer and Solectron's subsequent delivery of the finished product. This development represents, in effect, a step along the evolutionary path, away from the former practice of tossing designs over the wall to the manufacturing operation; now the wall itself is being torn down between customers and the companies, like Solectron, that do their manufacturing for them. Whatever this arrangement is called—"concurrent engineering" or "integrated product development"—it involves deeper collaborations between those who design the products and those who convert designs into low-cost, high-quality products. (See "The Brocade Initiatives," later in this chapter, for an in-depth example of Solectron's new relationships and deeper collaborations with its customers.)

Greater Value Through Information. When it comes to performance measurement, Solectron practices what it preaches, even when Solectron is the company being measured. On the customer's side of the company, Solectron uses a process that is an approximate mirror image of the measurement processes used on the supplier's side. A customer satisfaction index (CSI) is used in place of the supplier scorecard. The CSI contains five performance categories: quality, delivery, communications/responsiveness, service/flexibility, and technical support. The customer and Solectron mutually set goals in each category and assign weights to each category to reflect its relative importance to the customer. Solectron's actual performance and the assigned weights are used every week to calculate an overall grade ranging from A through F. When the grade falls below B-minus, a customer focus team submits an improvement plan to the customer, to get the customer's help in remedying the performance problem. Quarterly business reviews are also conducted, but in these reviews it is Solectron's performance that is evaluated by the customer, not the supplier's performance that is reviewed by Solectron. This customer-side review is more formal than the weekly CSI feedback process and tends to be a higher-level assessment that uses broader categories and addresses issues of a more strategic nature.

As an excellent example of the power of serendipity, Solectron's recent effort to integrate the many sites it acquired in the late 1990s has created another opportunity for the company to offer greater value to its customers. By the end of this period of aggressive acquisitions, Solectron owned about fifty manufacturing sites around the world, using about twelve different enterprise resource planning (ERP) systems. Instead of throwing out these very expensive systems, which in many cases were deeply embedded in the processes of the various sites, and starting over with a single standard system across all sites, Solectron was able to patch the systems together so that they could eventually "talk" to each other.

With further enhancements and refinements, this system, known as the "global data warehouse" (GDW), now enables Solectron to aggregate data from all its sites, particularly data concerning costs for different parts sold by different suppliers in different regions of the world. With this system, Solectron can extract very "granular" data (for example, information about inventory levels, prices, and demand for particular parts at a particular site) and aggregate the data by site, region, supplier, customer, and so on. Because the GDW can also update this information every few hours, users are able to track the rapid fluctuations in price that make the electronics business so volatile. The data—and the many applications Solectron has developed for analyzing, displaying, and reporting the information—can be accessed on the World Wide Web by managers, buyers, and others at each site, as an aid in guiding their decisions and actions. For example, the GDW enables users to track historical trends, project the demand for particular parts, negotiate prices with suppliers, reduce inventories by moving production to sites with excess inventory, and see where particular parts can be obtained at the best prices.

The system enables Solectron to tie together the many dispersed sites it acquired in the late 1990s, thus creating a globally integrated manufacturing capability. Because of the newly acquired sites' previous autonomy, cultures, and supplier bases, the company had not been able to shift production easily from one plant to another and thus take advantage of lower prices and idle capacity. The global data warehouse has changed all that. Solectron can now move production around to optimize costs across the company. In effect, this system has created the potential for a virtual "master scheduler in the sky" who can quickly shift production from one site to another and take advantage of short-term regional variations in prices for critical parts. The significance of the GDW for a globally dispersed organization like Solectron cannot be overstated. Steve Gearhart, Solectron's director of systems and data integration, succinctly captures the impact of the GDW: "In order to collaborate globally, you need to have a single version of the truth."

The most important use of the GDW is currently internal (to integrate sites and inform decision making), but Solectron is exploring the possibility of using this system to create new relationships with its customers. The GDW is like a dual-lens camera: it can provide customers both a telephoto lens, for looking all the way down the supply chain to the most detailed level, and a wide-angle lens, for looking at the big picture. The GDW can also be a very powerful strategic tool for Solectron's best customers. By opening up this system and sharing this information with customers, Solectron can enhance its value to its customers and become invaluable to them in the process.

The potential value of this system goes well beyond just the sharing of information. The GDW can help support the kinds of new services just described, especially where product design is concerned. As Vincent DePalma notes (2002, n.p.), "Selecting and acquiring the most cost-effective materials at the outset of a project is a crucial step in ensuring fast, efficient product development and delivery to customers." The GDW is a potentially critical tool in this strategically important process. It can help Solectron engineers work collaboratively with their customers to design products using less expensive and more readily available parts. Moreover, the GDW can help designers forecast trends, thereby enabling them to choose parts that are more likely to remain inexpensive and available throughout the entire life cycle of the products they design.

These new, closer relationships between Solectron and its customers, and with its suppliers as well, are built on a foundation of shared information and metrics. This situation raises an issue that is both intriguing and critical: How much information should Solectron share? How much is enough to maximize value and efficiency across the supply chain without at the same time breaching the boundaries of confidentiality and competitive advantage? In other words, to use the colorfully evocative language of the industry, how far should Solectron open the kimono to its customers (by disclosing, for example, how much the company is paying for parts—information its customers could use to bargain for lower prices from Solectron)? Conversely, how far should Solectron's customers open its kimono to Solectron?

The crucial question is how organizations involved in complex collaborations with other organizations can strike the appropriate balance between protecting proprietary information, on the one hand,

and sharing information to improve overall supply-chain effectiveness, on the other. How can these companies keep from completely blurring the boundaries between them? As customers, suppliers, and supply-chain facilitators like Solectron become more closely intertwined, this will be one of the most important challenges they will have to address to make these complex collaborations work.

Integrating Across the Global "Footprint"

While moving aggressively in these new directions, Solectron has also had to digest the large number of sites it acquired in the late 1990s. The acquisitions came fast and furious during that period. Before long, Solectron's global "footprint" had become far-flung and fragmented. The company was now made up of widely dispersed sites with different cultures, systems, and processes. Since that time, Solectron has worked hard to rein in the chaos left over from this era of acquisitions. As a result, consolidation is now a high priority; the company has divested itself of some of these sites and is doing a better job of integrating what is left. Common processes, metrics, and systems, including many of those already described (the supplier scorecard, quarterly business reviews, the global data warehouse, standard contracts) are critical elements of Solectron's integration strategy. Molding a common culture is another.

Integrating Through Culture. Our interviewees generally agreed about the elements of this common culture. Their specific words may have differed, but the themes were consistent. If we had to pick one word to describe this culture—a word that a number of our interviewees also picked—it would be "professional." What this word means to our interviewees is "hardworking," "fast-paced," "disciplined," "reality-focused," and "data- and performance-driven." The latter seems to be an especially critical element of the culture. One other element of the culture also deserves mention. Over the years, Solectron has been very success-oriented; the company is used to winning and being the best. Although this self-image has taken a bit of a beating in recent years, it still figures prominently in Solectron's attitudes and expectations, and is a position that the company is working hard to recapture.

Integrating Through Communication. Communication is another means Solectron uses to integrate across its far-flung global "footprint." Like most other widely dispersed organizations, Solectron use a variety of media to accomplish this purpose—phone, fax, e-mail, Web conferencing, and videoconferencing. Solectron personnel also travel a great deal to visit their sites and their regional suppliers. For example, one of our interviewees had been to China on Solectron business six times in the three months before our interview.

What is noteworthy about these efforts is not the technology or the means used—which are, after all, widely and commonly used—but the effort to use the technology well and with sensitivity, especially to collaborate across cultural boundaries. Solectron requires all employees to take a formal ethics training course to sensitize them to working with people of various backgrounds. This training, as described by Andrew Gomez, senior manager of procurement operations, is primarily focused on "appropriate behavior more than effective communications, but it does provide a baseline to people that words and actions can mean different things to different people." How this idea is implemented in Gomez's department is not necessarily typical throughout Solectron, but it does illustrate the kind of attention that needs to be paid to the challenges of cross-cultural communication in a global organization.

Gomez's team, at Solectron's site in Charlotte, North Carolina, is responsible for the deployment of the Web-based applications that the company has developed to support such procurement functions as replenishment, scheduling, and purchase-order transactions. These tools are used by the sites as well as by the company's suppliers, and they are a critical means of collaboration between them. Gomez's team defines business requirements, deploys the tools, and provides user training for the sites and suppliers.

From previous experience with cross-cultural collaboration, Gomez was aware of the potential "disconnects" that can occur when people who have different cultural backgrounds and native languages try to communicate with each other, especially when using e-mail. Therefore, as he began making plans for deploying the procurement tools in Asia, he looked for someone who had both cultural ties to the region (including appropriate language skills) and relevant business experience to serve as his team's link with Asia. He considered both criteria equally important.

Gomez was fortunate to find Choon Lee Ang, a native Malaysian who was working at the Solectron plant in Penang at the time. Ang also had more than ten years of experience in procurement and information technology, including some time as a user consultant. She was clearly a good match on both of Gomez's criteria. At the Penang plant she had played a similar role to the one Gomez had in mind for her in the United States: as the point of contact, the liaison, between the United States and Malaysia. In this role she had traveled to the United States fairly frequently, and so she was well suited to serve as the bridge between the two regions.

In her new role in the United States, Ang not only acts as a primary point of contact with the Penang site and the suppliers in the region but also serves as a consultant and as an informal, de facto trainer for others in her department who need to communicate with Asia. She has helped her colleagues learn the appropriate social norms for communicating with their contacts in Asia (for example, keep communications simple, clear, concise and frequent; formally address the person by his or her last name and social title; avoid cultural humor and discussions that are politically or religiously sensitive). Because Ang can also speak Malay and some Mandarin, she can act as a translator as necessary.

Gomez sums up Ang's wide-ranging impact and importance to the effective functioning of his department: "Others in the department have learned how to be more effective cross-cultural communicators through learning from and observing Choon Lee. Without her it would be considerably more difficult. She is a tremendous

asset and highly sought-after as a sounding board." This approach
has proved so successful that Gomez has replicated it for the other
regions that he and his team serve.

Across Solectron from Customer to Supplier. The challenges
of integration are not just geographical. An organization as complex
as Solectron needs to pay as much attention to integrating the many
organizations, divisions, and business units that make up the company as it does to integrating its numerous manufacturing sites
around the world. The separations among these units are primarily
functional because most units, other than the regional manufacturing sites, are within a few miles of each other in Silicon Valley.

Integration between the materials organization and the customer account management organization is especially important because, as these names suggest, together they span Solectron's primary
work process from one end of the company to the other, from supplier to customer and back again. As noted earlier, the materials
organization is responsible for everything concerning the materials that make up the customer's product. This division's work includes negotiating prices for parts, ordering and buying all parts and
supplies, assembling them into products, and making sure that all
these parts, supplies, and products are delivered to the appropriate
sites and customers for assembly or sale. The customer account
management organization is responsible for interacting with customers on both strategic and tactical issues as well as for developing
new business initiatives.

The all-important relationship between these two internal organizations is best seen in the context of the global account teams
that serve Solectron's largest and most strategically important customers. This team is made up of members from both organizations,
materials and customer account management, who collectively deal
with the entire range of customer issues, from negotiating contracts
to tracking orders for parts. The team is usually led by the representative from the account management organization, known as the
global account manager and referred to as the GAM. The GAM is

the primary contact with customers. The role of the GAM is to help customers with issues and problems as they come up and to look for revenue opportunities across all the services that Solectron offers— for example, by helping customers design their products around lower-cost materials and identify more efficient global supply chains. (David Moezidis, global account director for Brocade, the customer account that is the focus of the last third of this chapter, describes his role as being "the go-to person" who can help address all kinds of customer needs and help solve most problems. He also describes himself as the "one throat to choke," a phrase that reflects the often difficult challenges inherent in this highly important role.)

The customer liaison from the materials organization, referred to as the global account supply chain (GASC) director, is also an important member of this team, especially because material costs can account for as much as 50 percent of the cost of the final product and therefore has a major impact on the customer's (and Solectron's) profitability. The GASC director is primarily responsible for strategic and tactical issues involving materials and supply-chain management, from dealing with shortages of parts to coming up with major process improvements.

The GAM and the GASC often work closely together on the customer's site ("hand in glove" with the customer, in the words of Tim Griffin, GASC director for the Brocade account). All the team members spend much of their time on site and are usually provided with work areas, desks, phones, and e-mail access. Therefore, in the preceding descriptions of the functions of the customer account team, we see a high degree of integration between these two very critical units. This integration is primarily informal, however. It happens through personal, task-based interactions among team members from the two organizations as they collaborate on customer issues on site; it is not the product of formal mechanisms, common processes, and shared systems "back home" at Solectron. Several interviewees expressed some concern about this lack of integration and indicated that integration was likely to be a high priority in the near future.

Summary. In business these days, nothing stays the same for long. What has worked in the past may not work today, tomorrow, or the day after. That is why Solectron is exploring new ways to collaborate with its customers and suppliers—collaborations that are deeper, more intimate, and performance-based. In the rest of this chapter we examine this issue in more detail as we describe what may well be the prototype for Solectron's customer relationships from now into the future. The Brocade initiatives, discussed in the following section, illustrate how far Solectron has moved from the old outsourcing model to a new model of working hand in glove with its customers, blurring boundaries and meshing resources, people, and tasks in the pursuit of overlapping goals.

The Brocade Initiatives

Brocade Communication Systems, a NASDAQ 100 company headquartered in San Jose, is a survivor of the Silicon Valley technology crash of the early 2000s. The nature of the company's product—storage area networks (SANs)—has a lot to do with Brocade's success. SANs are designed to provide secure data storage and backup, in addition to disaster recovery, in the event of a system crash, a natural disaster, and even an act of terrorism, for organizations that need uninterrupted access to mission-critical information. The disruption experienced on September 11, 2001, by many businesses in the World Trade Center towers was less painful and dramatic than the loss of life, but it was serious nevertheless. Many companies never recovered from the financial impact of their lost data and systems. The need to back up data and critical applications in networked computers, off site and in secure locations, had never been as forcefully demonstrated before that fateful and painful day. Data backup and storage is the nature of Brocade's products and services. They include hardware, software, technology platforms, product support, and storage technology consulting services, mostly for large OEMs like Hewlett-Packard, Dell, IBM, and Hitachi Data Systems.

The company was founded in 1995 by former employees in the computer server industry, primarily from Sun Microsystems. They were soon joined by others from such technology leaders as Apple Computer, IBM, and Connor Peripherals. In recent years, a second generation of employees has joined the company, many from Brocade's long term-customer, Cisco. Brocade went public in 1999. In the words of one of our interviewees from Brocade, the company has been "wildly successful" since then; its stock split three times in two years, and for a while its revenues were doubling every quarter. Like most other companies in the world of high technology, however, Brocade hit a plateau in the early 2000s. Now the company, which employs more than 1,200 people worldwide, typically reports revenues of approximately $500 million per year. Matt Taylor, director of outsourcing for Brocade, describes the organization's culture as a blend of many other Silicon Valley cultures, reflecting the different companies represented in the résumés of their employees. The descriptors Taylor used—"aggressive," "accountable," "task-oriented," and "focused"—were consistent with the descriptions offered by others we interviewed.

The Solectron Connection

Brocade started out doing most of its own manufacturing in house, but, like many other high-tech companies, soon realized that manufacturing was not one of its core competencies and decided to outsource the manufacture of its printed circuit boards. Brocade then decided to go even farther by outsourcing all its manufacturing to a single source, taking advantage of the economies of scale and integrated services that a single supply-chain facilitator could offer. The company opened this area of its business to bids in 1997, and Solectron won the contract that marked the beginning of the Brocade-Solectron relationship. Soon thereafter, Brocade moved all its manufacturing to Solectron, just a short hop up the road in the heart of Silicon Valley. With this move, Solectron essentially became Brocade's manufacturing facility.

Brocade initially managed this relationship the same way most other customer-supplier relationships are managed in the electronics industry: it created the position of supply base manager to manage its supplier, and the supplier was Solectron. Everything was fine until the end of 1990s, when the industry hit an incredible spurt in technology growth. According to Matt Taylor, "Components were hard to find, people were hard to find. Everything was white-hot." Brocade management realized that Solectron might not be able to keep up with the accelerating demand for Brocade's products, especially because Solectron had other, bigger customers whose needs also had to be served. Brocade grew concerned that this potential bottleneck could impede its growth just as the company was gaining serious momentum.

At the same time, Brocade was less than completely satisfied with the performance of one of the Solectron plants responsible for manufacturing Brocade's enclosures (that is, the boxes for housing the company's systems). Brocade initially addressed this issue by becoming more tactical in its relationship with Solectron (for example, by monitoring the plant's performance very closely and holding daily meetings at the production facility in question). But it wasn't until Brocade considered taking its business elsewhere that the situation changed, significantly and rapidly.

In a move that reflected the new thinking at Solectron about supply-chain collaboration, Solectron responded decisively to the challenge by changing the Brocade supply chain and moving its manufacturing to a plant that could better meet Brocade's requirements. The process by which this issue was addressed was almost as important as the solution itself and helped sow the seeds for a new kind of relationship between the two companies.

"We didn't go tell them, 'We want to be here, and we want to be there,'" notes Taylor. Instead, "we told them, 'We have to fix this problem,' and they came back to us with the solution.'"

The transition took about six months and incredible effort on both sides, especially Solectron's. Since then, according to Taylor, everything was "much, much better."

For Brocade, this pivotal event did far more than resolve the immediate issue. It also inspired the company to explore a more collaborative approach, which was the perfect complement to the ideas percolating at the same time at Solectron. Thus, while Solectron was thinking about creating new kinds of relationships with its customers, Brocade was thinking about creating a new kind of relationship with Solectron and using it as a model for future relationships with its own suppliers and other contract manufacturers. Brocade recognized that to move beyond the one-way street of traditional customer-supplier relationships it would have to figure out a new way of working with contract manufacturers like Solectron and optimize its operations around this new model.

Matt Taylor's outsourcing group was then formed, to maximize Brocade's relationships with contract manufacturers and create an infrastructure for making these relationships work. In Brocade's view, this meant that while the company trusted that the contract manufacturers could do a better job than Brocade itself could in manufacturing its products, Brocade needed to help the manufacturers do a better job of serving Brocade—for example, by working out mutually acceptable schedules and collaboratively solving technical problems.

Solectron, of course, had been exploring its own version of this new collaborative approach to customer-manufacturer relationships, and so it quickly became an enthusiastic partner in this experiment. Brocade adopted a more facilitative approach in its relationship with Solectron, and the two companies worked collaboratively to figure out a way for Brocade to get the kind of service and performance it wanted without micromanaging the relationship. One of the first steps on this path toward a deeper, more effective collaboration between the two companies was to work jointly on various process improvements as well as on a number of other tactically and strategically important issues.

The partnership soon became fertile ground for further collaboration. Before long, the joint culture of deep collaboration that was rapidly developing between the two companies converged with a prior relationship between two key people and helped push the partnership to the next level. Jim Molzon, vice president of global logistics for Solectron, had met Matt Taylor several months earlier on a visit to Brocade to resolve a thorny service issue involving the two companies. Brocade had been impressed by Jim's personal attention, Jim had been impressed that Brocade had not "beat" him "over the head" about the issue. This and subsequent contacts between Jim and Matt over the next several months led them to realize that they shared an openness to new ideas and a willingness to explore new relationships, with significant upside potential.

The next opportunity was not long in emerging. Brocade had reached a critical point in its evolution from Silicon Valley start-up to mature corporation. The company's rapid growth meant that Brocade would have to build a significant logistics infrastructure and hire people to handle shipping and distribution of its products to its developing markets around the world. But Matt's boss, Nick Bacica, Brocade's vice president of operations, didn't want to invest in "people in non–real-value-added services," and so Matt turned to his colleague at Solectron for help. He asked Jim Molzon to figure out a way for Solectron to handle Brocade's logistical requirements and enable Brocade to take advantage of the lower shipping rates that Solectron could command because of the volume of business Solectron did with its shippers. Jim came up with a proposal, enlisted the support of his boss, and presented it to Matt, who in turn gained the support of Nick Bacica. The rest is history.

The Logistics Initiative

The most important element of the proposal called for a Solectron logistics employee to work full-time on site at Brocade. Jim Molzon tapped Glenn Ritter to fill the new role. Brocade agreed to pay Solectron for Glenn's services. The fee was set intentionally low for the first few months, with the proviso that if Brocade was happy with the arrangement, Brocade would voluntarily increase the amount to more closely match the value it felt the company was receiving. Brocade soon did increase the payment. Glenn, who at that point had been with Solectron for only two years, remained on Solectron's payroll, but in almost every other respect he acted as a Brocade employee and was treated as such by almost everyone with whom he worked. He had a desk, a phone, e-mail, and a Brocade employee badge. He was on site most days of the week, occasionally returning to Solectron to check in with his colleagues. It was understood from the beginning that this would be a temporary assignment and that Glenn would return full-time to Solectron after one year. It was also understood that Brocade would not try to "steal" him by actively recruiting him for a permanent position.

In this role, Glenn was acting, in essence, as Brocade's logistics manager. He was responsible for arranging the shipment of parts and subassemblies from plant to plant through the Brocade supply chain, and for getting the finished product to Brocade's customers around the world. He negotiated contracts, monitored costs, tracked orders, made sure bills got paid, and dealt with the requirements and challenges of moving goods and money from country to country. At least 50 percent of his job, in his estimation, was strategic. He was involved in special projects and initiatives—for example, developing performance metrics and analyzing and modeling different options for producing and moving parts. He also sat in on meetings at Brocade, to help formulate the strategic future of the Brocade supply chain.

Fortunately, Glenn did not have to do all of this on his own. He worked very closely with Nigel Johnson, his primary contact at Brocade. He could also tap into the vast experience, expertise, and resources of his home department whenever he needed to. He consulted frequently with Fred Hartung, his immediate supervisor at Solectron, and also spoke often with Jim Molzon, especially in the early stages, as he felt his way around his new role. At that point, he was the only Solectron logistics person on site at Brocade, but he had "a strong bench with lots of people and resources" to back him up. He could also plug into the Solectron logistics infrastructure—the standard practices and systems used by all

Solectron's logistics employees—so that he did not have to create this infrastructure from scratch for Brocade. For example, he used the same core group of carriers used by Solectron's logistics department and used the same carrier management practices regarding rates, contracts, pricing, and payment terms. In effect, the vast Solectron logistics capability—people, resources, and infrastructure—was channeled through him to Brocade by way of his continuing ties, both formal and informal, and the ongoing support of his department. In effect, he served as a virtual logistics department for Brocade. In his words, "They didn't just get a logistics guy, they got a whole company."

Glenn also had to get involved with a number of logistics issues involving a Solectron competitor that Brocade was using to fill some manufacturing needs. Since part of Glenn's role was to help review business processes, commercial invoices, and various shipping documents, he had access to highly sensitive information, especially about the price of parts and materials supplied by the competing company. The situation required a leap of faith on the part of Matt Taylor and others at Brocade and especially on the part of the competitor, which was fully informed of the new relationship between Brocade and Solectron and of Glenn's critical role in this relationship. Some people were initially leery of this arrangement—they "freaked," according to Matt. It wasn't long, however, before Glenn won them over.

He took it slow with the skeptics, listening closely to their concerns and not trying to tell them what to do; he was logical, task-focused, and service-oriented in his interactions with them. He gradually built relationships and trust as he learned how to navigate through this potentially dicey landscape. It also didn't hurt that he, Matt, and Nigel were soon able to offer proof of concept through a number of tactical "wins" (for example, they reduced trouble incidents from many per week to an average of one). Probably most important was the diligence and integrity that Glenn demonstrated in learning the boundaries of his role and of the information he routinely saw, and in the care he took not to cross those boundaries. He understood the potential consequences: "I'm like a Boy Scout around here. I never share anything I shouldn't. . . . I could ruin this relationship in an afternoon if I revealed certain things. . . . There is nothing I can share that would be worth messing this up."

After a few weeks, the concerns of the skeptics slipped away, and they, along with everyone else, began to treat Glenn as if he were a Brocade employee. The metrics that Glenn developed in collaboration with Nigel soon demonstrated that the logistics arrangement with Solectron was saving Brocade more money than it cost. That, plus the significant value-added services Glenn provided— such as modeling and analysis, developing metrics, and help in dealing with the strategic issues involved in the design and flow of Brocade's supply chain—cemented the deal. The experiment was no longer an experiment. Not only was it successful in its own right, it had also become a model for both companies for a new way of doing business with each other, and possibly with other supply-chain collaborators in the future.

Deep Collaboration in Action

Individuals like Glenn, Matt, and Jim were clearly critical to the success of the Brocade manufacturing and logistics initiatives, but it was the relationships and collaborations among everyone involved that made these initiatives work. One of the vehicles for this collaboration was the team of Solectron employees who worked on site at Brocade: the customer account management team. As described earlier, Solectron usually dedicates such a team to its largest customers, but Brocade was not one of them when the initiatives began. Arrangements for the Brocade account team differed from usual Solectron practice in another respect as well: the addition of a representative from Solectron's logistics department, Glenn. These exceptions to customary practice were significant indicators of the special relationship between the two companies.

Collaborative Processes. As another significant indicator of how special this relationship was, the team members worked very closely with their colleagues at Brocade. Other account teams also work closely with their customers, but the degree of collaboration between Solectron and Brocade was exceptional. For example, to help Solectron prepare for Brocade's version of the quarterly business review, Brocade would send its evaluation of Solectron's performance to the customer account team two weeks before the actual review. David Moezidis, the leader of the team, appreciated the consideration of his Brocade partners, who made sure that he and his team were not hit by unwelcome surprises at the meeting. It gave him and his team the opportunity to prepare by presenting possible solutions during the same meeting at which problems were raised. As a strong indication of just how intertwined the two partners had become, Jim Sutter, Brocade's primary contact for the manufacturing side of the collaboration, noted that this formal quarterly review process was probably not as necessary as it might have been in other relationships, because the Solectron team members received continuous feedback from their ongoing interactions and relationships with their Brocade counterparts.

Collaboration requires meetings—informal or formal, real or virtual—and this partnership was no exception. The collaborators met often, in various combinations, to share information, coordinate tasks, and solve problems. In addition, these meetings were frequently used as learning opportunities, to provide participants with a chance to reflect on the collaboration, how it was going, the problems they were encountering, what they could do to improve the process, and what they had learned that might be applicable to future projects with each other and with other partners. Early on, participants from both companies met to look at their prior experiences with their current and previous employers, to identify best practices and use them as guidelines for the new collaboration. Examples include Jim Sutter's weekly meetings with Solectron's on-site customer account team, and the meetings every two to three months among the people from both companies who were involved in the logistics initiative to review what they had been doing, how things were going, and how to take the relationship to the next level.

In addition, David Moezidis and Matt Taylor jointly sponsored a formal briefing every year, which turned out to be an excellent forum for dialogue between the two companies. The forum, referred to as the "Hayes Mansion meetings" (and named after the location where they were held), were usually attended by five to seven vice presidents and other senior-level managers from the two companies, as well as by some of the key operational-level people involved in the collaboration. The purpose of the forum was to address high-level strategic issues in the developing relationship. The agenda typically included such items as an overview of the activities and developments of the past year, a survey of what the two companies had learned from the initiatives, a discussion of areas that needed improvement, and suggestions for what should be the focus of the next year. This annual forum was valued not just for the substantive content covered in its meetings but also because it provided an opportunity to celebrate the successes of the initiative and of the deep collaborations between the two companies.

Relationship Building.   Both sides of the partnership also paid a great deal of attention to relationship building. Clearly, the decision makers at both Solectron and Brocade understood the critical role of co-location and face-to-face interactions in relationship building; for example, the members of the Brocade customer account team spent much of their time on site at Brocade, and Brocade provided them with work space and made it clear to everyone at Brocade that they were to be treated like Brocade employees. Brocade was not the only location for face-to-face relationship building: Jim Sutter of Brocade sent one of his staff members, Joel Sherwood, to the Solectron factory in Columbia, South Carolina, for six months to learn Solectron's systems, develop processes for linking the plant with Brocade, and establish relationships with Solectron people at the plant that could be helpful to him after his residency was over. It made his job a lot easier after he returned to Brocade—he knew Solectron's systems, how they worked, and whom to go to for information or help in resolving problems between the two sites.

It turned out that this sojourn was not just a one-way transaction. Solectron people at the plant often asked Joel about Brocade and about how best to work with their Brocade counterparts back in Silicon Valley. As Joel notes, "They used me as much as I used them." The bottom line was that this arrangement enabled both partners to learn how to work more effectively with each other. They used this approach at every opportunity; for example, Brocade people were often on site in Penang or visited frequently, and Jim Sutter and his Solectron counterpart, Tim Griffin, often traveled together to the Solectron plants for the explicit purpose of strengthening their relationship. Jim sums up this strategy of "mutual co-location" (our expression, not theirs) by noting that they made "a concerted effort to take time to form a really good partnership to leverage each other's strengths."

Summary.   By all accounts, this was a very successful effort. Brocade was able to keep its costs down and focus on its core competencies, Solectron made money, and both parties had the opportunity to develop a new, more collaborative way of working with each other and with other potential supply-chain collaborators. Keith McDonald, Solectron's corporate vice president of global accounts, describes the Brocade arrangement as "a premiere example of a collaborative relationship hitting on all cylinders." To mark the success of this relationship, Brocade's CEO Award was presented to Solectron in June 2002 "for demonstrating outstanding performance across the entire supply chain." Only one supplier or outsourced manufacturer receives the prestigious award each year.

What made this work? Can this kind of success be replicated by other organizations, or is it largely dependent on the serendipitous convergence of a handful of very rare and special people with unique qualities? In the next chapter, we try to answer that question by identifying the steps that Solectron took to create closer relationships with its customers and suppliers in general, and especially with Brocade, the company's early partner in exploring new directions in innovation and deep collaboration.

Chapter Six

What the Solectron Initiatives Tell Us About Collaboration Across the Supply Chain

In the last chapter, we described what Solectron is doing to strengthen its relationships with customers and suppliers. In recent years the company has moved away from the old outsourcing model built around sequential hand-offs up and down the supply chain to an approach that features closer collaboration with supply-chain partners. Solectron no longer keeps its best customers and suppliers at arm's length, viewing them only as companies to buy from and sell to. Instead, Solectron now sees them as potential partners and collaborators. In this chapter we examine how Solectron executes this strategy, and what actions that suggests for other organizations with similar strategies and goals. Table 6.1 summarizes the action steps that will be identified in the pages that follow.

Phase I: Setting the Stage

Solectron has invested considerable time and effort to set the stage for deeper collaborations with its suppliers and customers. Like John Deere and Radica, the company has articulated and promoted a strategic vision and culture that support collaboration across boundaries. What is unique about this case, however, is how much attention has been paid to the development of a collaboration infrastructure. Even more unique is how Solectron uses this infrastructure to support its collaborative processes.

Table 6.1. Action Steps from the Solectron Case

Phase	Action Step
Phase I: Setting the Stage	*Promote a strategic vision of supply-chain collaboration* through written and spoken words and actions
	Develop an organizationwide infrastructure that supports collaboration through
	Information systems and metrics
	Contracts
	Standardized practices
Phase II: Getting Started with Specific Projects	*Find partners with compatible performance-based cultures*
	Management actively and visibly supports projects
	By developing trust and taking visible risks
	By providing autonomy to participants
	Put the right people in the right place
	Create liaison roles
	Link the liaisons in collaborative pairs
	Fill liaison roles with people who have good lateral skills (that is, who can communicate across geographical and functional cultures, provide customer service and more, demonstrate integrity, and inspire trust)

Phase III:
Creating the Infrastructure

Adapt pre-existing governance and management practices to specific projects (for example, by creating an account management team and providing lots of autonomy to on-site participants)

Develop and use performance metrics for strategic and political purposes (for example, as early indicators of success in order to build support)

Phase IV:
Doing the Work

Establish norms for communicating across cultures and organizations, by using liaisons to establish and teach norms and by sharing information

Build relationships through travel and face-to-face interaction

Learn from doing

Go for early wins

Promote a Strategic Vision of Supply-Chain Collaboration

The most important step taken by Solectron management has been to publicly promote a strategic vision of supply-chain collaboration and to act on this vision by pursuing and supporting projects like the Brocade initiatives. The citations in the last chapter from Solectron's annual report and from Solectron executives demonstrate the company's commitment to this vision. These statements also serve the purpose of promoting and reinforcing this vision throughout the company. If our interviews are any indication, Solectron management at all levels buys into this vision and is not reluctant to articulate what this means for management and the people being managed. Solectron clearly promotes its strategic vision via the written and spoken word, and, as the Brocade initiatives demonstrate, by deeds as well.

The data- and performance-driven culture we described in the last chapter is one of the most important elements of this strategic vision. The systems, metrics, and processes we also described in the previous chapter helped create this culture. Collectively, they comprise an infrastructure that supports and drives performance, particularly in collaborations with supply-chain partners.

Develop an Organizationwide Infrastructure That Supports Collaboration

The Solectron case is a good example of the increasing role of structure as collaborations become more complex. This case is far more complex than either of our preceding two cases, and so the degree of what we loosely define as "structure" is much greater. The nature of this structure is also different—that is, metrics in the form of supplier scorecards and customer satisfaction indexes; integrated information systems, such as the global data warehouse and Web-based procurement tools; detailed formal contracts with both customers and suppliers; and the standardization of these practices, systems, and processes. Despite these differences, the action steps that emerge from the Solectron case have an effect similar to that of the effects identified in the previous cases. That is, the action steps reduce uncertainty and increase predictability, thereby making complex collaborations less complex and more manageable. They make it easier for those involved to get a handle on the many issues, problems, and challenges they have to face in order to make these collaborations work.

Of all of our cases, the Solectron case best illustrates the role of structure in enhancing collaborative relationships. As we noted in the last chapter, Solectron has moved aggressively in the last few years to impose more structure on the previously informal, relationship-based nature of its industry. In effect, Solectron has tried to balance its earlier dependence on "handshakes" and individual personalities and styles with information, standardization, and formal agreements. This is what people at Solectron mean when they talk about creating a more "professional" culture, a critical element in their strategy for moving from contract manufacturer to global supply-chain facilitator. Let us take a look at the various elements of Solectron's structure to see how it is used, not to replace relationships between organizations and the people within them, but to enhance these relationships and help them work more effectively.

Information Systems and Metrics.   Information, and systems for processing and deploying this information, play a critical role in Solectron's push to create new relationships with suppliers and customers. Solectron's managers recognize that this involves more than just data and technology. They realize that the value of information is greatly enhanced when it is embedded within a collaborative process. For example, the information generated by the Supplier Council is the product of discussions among executives from Solectron and their top suppliers to identify critical issues, solve problems, and speculate on trends. One of the potential uses of the global data warehouse is to work with customers to interpret the implications of the information and understand how it can be used in product engineering. Similarly, the full value of the supplier scorecard and the customer satisfaction index emerges from the use of these two instruments in the give-and-take environment of the quarterly business reviews, where Solectron works with suppliers to help improve their performance and with customers to help improve its own performance. The point is that all these systems and metrics are embedded in a collaborative process where information often serves as the starting point for discussions, not as the final word. These discussions not only help Solectron solve problems and address other issues of mutual interest but also develop and strengthen relationships in the process.

Contracts. The same can be said about how Solectron uses contracts, especially with its suppliers. To repeat Paul DeMand's quote from the last chapter: "Life is compromise and negotiation. The document is a starting point, but we can be open and flexible, depending on how serious the issue is, of course." Good, long-term relationships with reliable suppliers are more important than occasional problems with delivery dates and cancelled orders. Solectron recognizes how important these relationships can be when circumstances change and the shoe is on the other foot. The company also recognizes that good relationships require more than just a piece of paper and a formal process.

Therefore, contracts sometimes serve as the basis for further discussion and negotiation, not as the final word. Contracts, by spelling out assumptions, understandings, and interpretations in advance, help both to focus discussion on what is really important and to avoid endless bickering about peripheral details. Paul DeMand's boss, Eddie Maxie, vice president of global supply management, refers to the "delicate dance" that is often required to keep discussions going with suppliers until difficult issues are resolved, even issues that are unequivocally spelled out in the terms and conditions of the contract. The bottom line for Solectron is that although contracts are necessary, there are times when they can be viewed as a starting point for the "delicate dance" of compromise and negotiation, not as a replacement. Of course, contracts are necessary for spelling out the boundaries of this dance, but if the issues are not too serious and there is some room for compromise, the "dancers" can improvise new steps in the process and learn how to dance better with their partners. And we all know that good connections between dancers produce better performances.

Standardized Practices. The role of structure in Solectron's relationships with its customers and suppliers is to support the relationships, not to serve as a substitute. The impact of such practices, processes, and systems as the global data warehouse, the supplier scorecard, the customer satisfaction index, supplier contracts, and the quarterly business reviews is to reduce uncertainty and arbitrariness, making it easier for everyone to focus on the most important issues. Standardizing these practices multiplies their effects. Suppliers, for example, know that they will be subject to the same metrics and review processes, regardless of the buyers they work with and the factories they supply. Similarly, standard templates for contracts define terms and identify issues that are important for all orders—cost, delivery dates, warranties, and so on. Suppliers know what to expect and can therefore build relationships that are based on dimensions open to discussion and over which they can exert some influence. Neither the suppliers nor the buyers have to waste time arguing over definitions or issues not central to their principal tasks.

Summary. Relationships with customers and suppliers are critical to Solectron. They drive the business, are the source of new business, and help the company manage costs. That is why Selectron has devoted so much time and effort in recent years to developing an organizationwide infrastructure for supporting these relationships. This is a cornerstone of Solectron's strategy for making the transition from contract manufacturer to global supply-chain facilitator.

This infrastructure both reflects the company's performance-focused culture and reinforces it. The infrastructure and the culture together help set the stage for all collaborations and provide a context for doing business without boundaries. With this foundation, Solectron was ready to move forward with one of its most far-reaching manifestations of this new strategic direction: the Brocade initiatives.

Phase II: Getting Started with Specific Projects

Like the John Deere case, the Solectron-Brocade collaborations demonstrate how important it is to find like-minded partners. This case also suggests certain characteristics that partners should have in common. Compatibility of goals and capabilities is just as important in this case as in the John Deere case. Compatible goals and capabilities are the sine qua non of supply chains—that is, customers develop and market products, and companies like Solectron manufacture them—so incompatibility should not be an issue. If it were, the links in the supply chain would soon break apart. Compatibility of cultures, by contrast, is not as obvious. Therefore, unless the partners pay close attention to this issue, it can be a significant barrier to successful supply-chain collaborations, especially the kind of deep collaboration that Solectron sees as the cornerstone of its future.

Find Partners with Compatible Performance-Based Cultures

Brocade shares Solectron's uncompromising focus on performance. In fact, the Solectron-Brocade partnership might not have worked as well if Solectron had entered into this partnership with an older, more traditional company. Brocade is anything but old and traditional. A young, entrepreneurial company on the way up, the company is clearly a reflection of the Silicon Valley culture that spawned it. Brocade has outsourced almost all its manufacturing since the company's earliest days, and so there wasn't an entrenched legacy of manufacturing to get in the way of the new manufacturing collaboration with Solectron: no pre-existing manufacturing culture to overcome, no turf to defend, and no competing ideas about how manufacturing should be done.

Brocade's entrepreneurial and forward-looking nature was consistently mentioned in our interviews with the Solectron participants. They described Brocade as "innovative," "open to new ways of doing business," "informal, relaxed, but success-driven," "not looking to protect turf," and "nimble and able to drive things through." Solectron's Tim Griffin describes Brocade in terms that echo the words used by several Solectron interviewees to describe their own company: "They are open to trying new things. They are pretty demanding as well. They hold us accountable for results. We have to think things through. We can't get by with a lot of fluff. Our ideas have to have substance and be logical."

Clearly, both partners had to take a very big leap of faith for their collaboration to move to the next level. The reason both companies were willing to take this leap of faith was not because of any idealistic belief in the value of collaboration for its own sake, but because both partners believed that they would make more money by doing so—maybe not right away, but surely soon enough to make the effort and the risk worthwhile. They were drawn to each other because of their mutual interest in exploring new approaches to improving their performance: for Brocade, cost savings and reliable delivery of parts and materials; for Solectron, new revenue opportunities. Both companies realized that new kinds of relationships with their partners were a potential source of these improvements. Both companies were open to trying new things, willing to take calculated risks, and nimble enough to respond rapidly to emerging opportunities.

Management Actively and Visibly Supports Projects

Because the Solectron-Brocade collaborations were initiated by high-level managers in both organizations, gaining top management's support for the projects was not an issue. Therefore, the key actions, besides actually getting the projects started, revolved around what the managers did to actively promote and support them. One of the most important steps was to develop a joint culture for the project that enabled the two partners to quickly develop trust and respect for each other.

Developing Trust by Taking Visible Risks. While the two partners' common focus on performance and the compatibility of their cultures helped get their partnership started, mutual trust between them is what kept it moving forward. Just about everyone we spoke to mentioned the highly collaborative joint culture as one of the primary reasons for the partnership's success. This joint culture of mutual trust and respect developed quickly and made it easy for everyone to interact with candor and openness, to share information, and to trust each other's good intentions, integrity, and competence.

How were the partners able to develop mutual trust so quickly? Part of the answer lies in each company's willingness to take risks that unequivocally demonstrated this trust, such as Brocade's "opening the kimono" to Solectron, and Jim Molzon's willingness to let Brocade decide how much to pay for Glenn's services. Just as important, perhaps even more so, was how the management of each company supported those directly responsible for the project's success: the Solectron and Brocade employees involved in the project's day-to-day tasks.

Providing Autonomy to Participants. One of the most visible manifestations of this support was the degree of autonomy Jim Molzon gave Glenn to deal with the day-to-day needs of his client. In Glenn's words, Jim was "very hands-off" in how he dealt with him; Glenn noted that Jim did "what he [needed] to do at an executive level to put the pieces into place. . . . 'We want to do this, go do it, and talk to me three weeks later to tell me if things are going OK.'" Glenn reported that Jim got involved when he needed to, but "as long as [I was] delivering, he [let] me run with it."

Even with all this autonomy, Glenn knew that he was not out there alone; he had a lifeline back to his base at Solectron. He was expected to check in regularly and could get advice and assistance whenever he needed it. This was especially helpful in the first few months of his engagement at Brocade. It was a new type of assignment for him, and so Jim and Fred Hartung, Glenn's immediate supervisor at Solectron, made sure to let him know that they were not cutting the ties. They made a special effort at the beginning to stay in touch and encourage him to come back for help, resources, and so on, whenever he needed. Glenn wasn't afraid to ask for help and took advantage of this support as he learned the boundaries of his new position.

This combination of autonomy and support offered the best of both worlds to Brocade. Glenn could act on his own initiative to deal with issues as they came up, or he could tap in to Solectron's deep "bench" of people and resources when the issues required more than he could provide on the spot. This flexibility gave Glenn ample opportunity to demonstrate both his integrity in how he handled his access to sensitive information and his value to Brocade in his role as their de facto logistics manager. Trust in Glenn, in his role, and in the expanding relationship with Solectron soon followed.

Brocade's management also provided critical support for the collaborations with Solectron. The Brocade managers' very willingness to open up their organization to Solectron and stake so much of the company's future on Solectron's performance and integrity said a lot about their support for these ventures. How this support played out at the tactical and operational levels, particularly in terms of support for the Solectron employees on site, is especially instructive. This support was apparent not only in physical and formal arrangements—desks, offices, phones, badges, e-mail addresses, and so on—but in the way the Solectron employees were treated by Brocade management. David Moezidis describes how Nick Bacica, Brocade's vice president of operations, promoted and supported his role throughout Brocade, "up and down the [hierarchical] chain, in . . . staff meetings and in . . . day-to-day interactions with [the] team." According to David, Bacica publicly stated in several meetings that David was his "vice president of manufacturing" (David also notes that he appreciated the "promotion to VP"). Bacica described him, according to David, as "the guy he goes to whenever he has manufacturing issues or questions. . . . He is like a member of my organization, an extension of my staff." He pointedly made this statement to his team at Brocade as well as in meetings with Solectron's executives. Not surprisingly, David describes this as "very empowering." He also adds that this support played a major role in the development of the joint culture of mutual trust.

Put the Right People in the Right Place

This case has much in common with the other two cases in terms of what they all say about the importance of creating liaison roles, linking these roles where appropriate, and putting the right people in these roles. This case also provides additional insight into what we mean by "the right people."

Create Liaison Roles. The connection between the Solectron plants in North Carolina and Malaysia presented challenges similar to the connection between the product designers in Dallas and the engineers in Hong Kong in the Radica Bass Fishin' game project. In the Solectron case, Choon Lee Ang is Solectron's version of Lam, and Andrew Gomez is Solectron's version of Bob Davids, at least in this respect. Like Bob, Andrew was aware of the important role of cultural sensitivity in communications between the two plants and dealt proactively with this issue by assigning Choon Lee Ang to act as a liaison between the two sites. Like Lam, Ang had a foot in each of the cultures represented at each site and was fluent in both English and Malay.

Link the Liaisons in Collaborative Pairs. The Brocade-Solectron collaborations required a different approach. There were two distinct organizations involved, the organizations had to work together very closely, people needed to communicate back and forth frequently, and they often had to address issues jointly. This was a much more complex situation than the one just described. The nature of the tasks and their context called for a deeper, more intimate, immediate, and continuous collaboration between the two companies. One liaison person linking the two organizations would not have been enough, just as it was not enough in the later projects at Radica after the acquisition of the company in the United Kingdom.

This situation called instead for the formation of collaborative pairs, which is of course what happened, the pairs either emerging naturally from the tasks on which people worked or intentionally created for specific purposes. The Brocade-Solectron collaborations were built on the foundation of collaborative pairs: between Jim Molzon from Solectron and Matt Taylor from Brocade, to get the ball rolling on the logistics initiative, and between Glenn and Nigel Johnson, to keep it rolling. Other collaborative pairs were also critical—for example, between Matt Taylor and David Moezidis, who provided high-level coordination and oversight of all the Brocade-Solectron initiatives.

That said, it is important to note that the collaborative pairing of Glenn and Nigel soon evolved into a single liaison linking both sites, with Glenn serving in the liaison role. Two factors made this possible: Glenn's having built relationships and trust among the many people at Brocade with whom he interacted, and Nigel's having left Brocade several months into the initiative. This suggests that the decision concerning the structure and nature of the liaison role(s)—that is, the choice of whether to use a single liaison or collaborative pairs—should be revisited as conditions and relationships change.

Fill Liaison Roles with People Who Have Good Lateral Skills. Again like the other cases, the Solectron case demonstrates the importance of putting the right people in liaison roles—that is, people who have good lateral skills. But this case adds some new wrinkles to our understanding of these skills. To better understand what we mean by lateral skills, let us look more closely at two of the liaison people just mentioned: Choon Lee Ang and Glenn Ritter. By all accounts, both were very effective in this critical role. Most of the others already mentioned also demonstrated good lateral skills, but the particular conditions of Choon Lee Ang's and Glenn's roles presented special challenges and put greater demands on their lateral skills than was true for the others. Therefore, we can extrapolate from what we know of their behavior and characteristics to flesh out further what we mean by these very important skills.

Choon Lee Ang, like Lam, was able to communicate across both cultural and functional boundaries. With one foot firmly planted in the West and the other in Asia, she was able to bridge differences in both culture and language. In the years to come, as more and more manufacturing moves to Asia and other areas with lower labor costs, the ability to span international cultures will become even more important.

She was also able to bridge what is often the most vexing cultural gap of all: between those who develop new technologies and tools and those for whom the technologies are developed. Effectively bridging this gap is one of the best predictors of a system's ultimate success (Klein and Ralls, 1995). With her several years of experience in both information technology and procurement, along with her experience as an information technology user consultant, she was ideally suited to link the developers of the Web-based procurement tools with the eventual users of these tools. Her lateral skills enabled her to collaborate across the different cultures of Asia and North America, as well as across the different worlds of "techie" and user.

Elsewhere we have discussed at some length the qualities that enable technology developers, user consultants, and other "techies" to work effectively with technology users (Mankin, Cohen and Bikson, 1996). One of these qualities is cross-cultural communication, where "culture" is defined by the different professional cultures, or "thought worlds" (Dougherty, 1992), associated with different functions (information technology, engineering, marketing, and so on). Choon Lee Ang possessed this quality. Another quality we discussed in our earlier book is an orientation to customer service. Glenn provides an excellent example of what we mean by this and how it adds to our growing understanding of the concept of lateral skills.

Glenn was clearly a master of customer service. Everyone we interviewed about the Brocade-Solectron collaborations pointed to Glenn as one of the most important reasons for the success of the logistics initiative. Our respondents were also very consistent in their descriptions of those qualities that they thought made him so effective in this role. His background as an entrepreneur (he had run an import-export business in African art) and as an avid rock climber impressed several people, although they were less clear about how these experiences may have contributed to his success. The relevance of the other qualities they cited is easier to see; "steady temperament," "good communicator," and "smart" were the descriptors used by most of our interviewees.

Several of the other qualities mentioned by a number of people seem to fit together into a coherent pattern. Different people used different words, but the overall picture is consistent: "He is open to working with others, especially customers, and is sensitive to their needs and concerns"; "He wants to help, to understand others' issues and concerns so that he can serve them better." According to Jim Molzon, "Glenn does a really good job of listening to the client. He really hears what they have to say." Jim also notes that Glenn recognizes when he needs help and is not shy about seeking out this help when he has to.

We have previously used the personality construct of empathy (see Chapter Two) to capture the essence of this pattern, and it seems to apply to Glenn as well. But it's more than that—it's viewing the people you work with as customers and doing your best to serve them well. He is able to put himself in his customers' place.

Because he can internalize their needs and make them his own, he understands their needs and can serve them better. This is empathy in the service of customer service.

The qualities that may be most important, especially for an interorganizational collaboration such as this, and those that were most often cited, are integrity and the ability to inspire trust. Given Glenn's access to potentially confidential information, it is not difficult to see why these qualities were so important in this sensitive role. As we saw in the last chapter, Glenn was very careful about the boundaries of his role. He even had the good sense to check with others when in doubt about the sensitivity of information he came across in the execution of his tasks and responsibilities. It didn't take him long to dispel any concerns others might have had about the arrangement. In Matt Taylor's words, "Glenn knows how to work with people. . . . Jim [Molzon] did a good job in putting the right person in the job."

Phase III: Creating the Infrastructure

For an organization that is as reliant on formal structure as Solectron—as seen, for example, in the company's use of supplier scorecards, quarterly business reviews, the global data warehouse, and formal contracts—the company apparently created surprisingly little formal structure for its collaboration with Brocade. Examples of formal structure were rarely mentioned in our interviews dealing specifically with the Brocade-Solectron collaborations. The emphasis in most interviews clearly reflected the other "thread" of our action framework: relationships, people, and culture (rather than structures, formal processes, metrics, and systems). In fact, several interviewees commented on the general informality and lack of structure. For example, in answer to our question about the existence of a contract for the logistics initiative, Fred Hartung of Solectron said, "If there is one, I haven't seen it. We agreed through e-mails about what we would deliver and what it would cost."

Reflecting on the high level of trust between the two companies, he added, "With anybody else, we would have developed a contract." In addition, there was considerably less discussion of systems and technology in the Brocade-Solectron interviews than there was in the other Solectron interviews.

One should not conclude, however, that structural factors did not play a major role in the success of the Brocade-Solectron collaborations. Solectron's substantial infrastructure of metrics, systems, and standardized practices was important to the people at Brocade and was a primary reason why Brocade asked Solectron to handle its manufacturing and logistics needs in the first place. This infrastructure is built in to the very fabric of Solectron and is embedded in almost everything the company does. Because of this highly developed, pre-existing structure, the Solectron-Brocade participants did not feel an urgent need to develop much in the way of additional structure specifically for their work. To serve most of the infrastructure needs of the Brocade initiatives, all they had to do was adapt existing structures, systems, and practices rather than build them from scratch for these particular initiatives.

Adapt Pre-existing Governance and Management Practices to Specific Projects

The on-site customer account team offers a good example of how Solectron structures were adapted to support the Brocade collaborations. Creating these teams and placing them on site is standard Solectron practice to serve the needs of its best customers. It is hard to imagine the Brocade initiatives working as well without this team. The team members were generally available in person to provide information, answer questions, and respond quickly to the needs of their Brocade colleagues. Because they were on site, the team members were also able to gain a deeper and more immediate firsthand understanding of their clients' needs and circumstances. Most important, by working as a team rather than just as individuals, they were able to coordinate their efforts and share among themselves what they learned about how best to serve their customers.

This team also fulfilled a very important symbolic function. Brocade was not a large customer when the initiatives began, and so the presence of a substantial on-site team was an important indication of Solectron's commitment to this burgeoning relationship. The special status of this relationship, as symbolized by the team, probably made it easier for people like Glenn, for example, to gain quick acceptance at Brocade.

The leadership approach was also consistent with standard practice at Solectron. In addition, however, it reflected subtle modifications of degree to accommodate the special circumstances of the project. Leadership in general at Solectron was similar to what we saw at Radica—hands off and facilitative when it could be, directive and firm when it had to be. The directive side can be seen in the unequivocal commitment of senior management to building a more professional culture based on standard metrics, processes, and systems. With that in place, managers were able to trust their people to function in a manner consistent with the culture and did not have to monitor them constantly to make sure that they were doing what they were supposed to be doing. In other words, they firmly believed that when people internalize the culture, they can manage themselves.

Managers acted on this belief by focusing on how to facilitate the performance of those they managed—for example, by providing resources, direction, feedback, and coaching—rather than on directing their behavior. People are the key to making this work, according to Eddie Maxie. "You can't do any of this without good people," he notes. "Can they work in an unstructured environment? Are they self-motivated? Are they trustworthy? If you keep people focused on the deliverables and the goals on the scorecard, then you don't have to supervise them as closely to get the work done."

This facilitative approach to management was especially evident in the Brocade initiatives and is reflected in Glenn's comments, cited earlier in this chapter, about the results-focused, hands-off leadership style of his boss, Jim Molzon. As we saw in the last chapter, Glenn was given an extraordinary amount of autonomy to "run with it" in his role as Solectron's logistics manager and as a liaison for Brocade. This degree of autonomy enabled him to deal with Brocade's logistics needs at the point of action in a timely and appropriate manner.

Develop and Use Performance Metrics

Glenn used his autonomy well. On his own initiative, and with Matt's support and Nigel's help, he developed systems for assessing the impact and value of the logistics services he was providing to Brocade. This is one of the first things he did in his new role. These systems tracked such measures as number of trouble instances, average cost per shipment, and number of daily shipments. Other measures were added along the way. The metrics soon provided clear indications of performance improvement and cost savings, indications that helped affirm the value of the initiative in its critical early stages. We can see that these metrics not only were important for tracking and improving performance but also served a critical political function: building support for the initiative at Brocade by demonstrating its value. This effort was so successful that it suggests an action step in its own right: developing measures to provide early indicators of success, in order to build support and commitment, strengthen the collaboration, and lay the foundation for further progress. Of course, this also means that expectations have to be reasonable so that early assessments encourage further collaboration instead of discouraging continued effort. (We will return to this issue when we discuss carrying out project tasks and learning from the results, later in this chapter.)

Summary

The few instances described here are not the only examples of how the participants created infrastructure for the Solectron-Brocade collaborations. Other examples include Glenn's use of Solectron's list of standard carriers and the company's standard practices for billing rates, terms, and conditions, and Matt Taylor's and Jim Sutter's regular access to inventory reports generated by Solectron's global data warehouse. Despite these examples, it seems as if explicit efforts to develop infrastructure for the initiatives were limited. This raises the question of why this was so, especially given Solectron's focus on these issues in general.

A possible explanation is that Solectron already had a substantial infrastructure in place for supporting relationships with all its suppliers and customers. This structure was pre-existing and did not need to be reinvented for the collaborations with Brocade. Another possible explanation, not inconsistent with the one just proposed, is that the Brocade-Solectron initiatives were still modest in size and in their early stages when we conducted our interviews. For the most part, the initiatives involved only a handful of people, in relative terms, who were co-located, knew each other well, and generally got along. Therefore, the people involved in the initiative were able to perform most tasks and address most issues on the spot, as they came up, by talking to each other and to other colleagues at the two companies. It is possible that the initiatives were still of manageable size, scope, and complexity at the time and did not require more explicit and formal structures. If collaborations between these two companies develop further, they may have to focus more attention on enhancing their infrastructure, to help manage these larger and more ambitious initiatives.

Phase IV: Doing the Work

For the most part, the phase IV action steps for this case are similar to those that emerged from our analyses of the other two cases, although with some added details. This case also adds a new action step, "Go for early wins," which fits well with the steps already identified in the previous cases concerning learning from doing and

modifying plans and goals on the basis of these learnings. Taken together, these action steps provide an integrated, holistic approach
to doing the substantive work that is the focus and purpose of the
collaborations.

Establish Norms for Communicating Across Cultures and Organizations

Solectron's far-flung "footprint" reflects the increasingly global
nature of the EMS industry. Therefore, communication technologies play an essential role at Solectron, especially in integrating
its many sites, suppliers, and customers around the world. As the
Radica case demonstrated, however, the particular systems and
technology may be less important than how they are actually used.

The example presented in the last chapter, involving the link
between sites in North Carolina and Malaysia, illustrates that it is
the matrix of processes, norms, roles, and competencies within
which these systems are embedded that makes them effective.
Technology was a necessary but not sufficient condition for effective communications with Penang. It was Andrew Gomez's social/
micro-organizational designs that transformed the hardware and
software into a functional technology—into a system for communicating effectively across time, distance, and especially culture. He
created the liaison role in Charlotte, placed Choon Lee Ang in that
role, and made sure that everyone knew what her role was as well
as the implications for their communications with the Penang
plant. He also used Ang to help develop the cross-cultural communication skills of everyone on his team. Before long, everyone had
learned and internalized the new norms and expectations and
developed the skills and sensitivity that transformed the communications equipment into an effective communications technology.

In the Brocade-Solectron collaborations, communications technology was less of an issue because most of the participants were co-
located on site at Brocade, and the Solectron headquarters was

nearby. Therefore, the principal communications issue concerned the sharing of information, not the transmitting of information back and forth between distant sites. The parameters of this issue are described by Matt Taylor: "We are open and honest with them in our communication. We don't hold things back. We want to understand what measurements drive them because we want them to be successful. . . . They are fairly open-book with us around their costs, and we are fairly open-book with them about what we need from them."

This is the "open kimono" in operation. What made it work for Brocade and Solectron are the action steps described in this chapter, none more important than those involving mutual trust and the strong relationships on which this mutual trust has been built, brick by brick.

Build Relationships Through Travel and Face-to-Face Interaction

How did the two companies build these relationships? Perhaps the most important action step of all was their use of face-to-face interactions to build the relationships that were, ultimately, the foundation for everything else. Solectron managers strongly believe in using face-to-face interactions as much as possible to perform tasks, build relationships, and share what they have learned to improve their performance. We base this conclusion not just on specific actions taken in their collaboration with Brocade but also on the way in which they do business and perform tasks in general. One of the clearest illustrations of this belief is Solectron's policy of assigning account management teams to work on site for the company's most strategically important customers. This enables Solectron to work directly with their customers. These on-site teams also enable the team members to coordinate their work face to face, to better serve their customers.

In fact, travel is unavoidable in the EMS business, and because Solectron sites are spread virtually all over the world, Solectron employees probably travel more than most. Management recognizes the importance of frequent travel to meet face to face with suppliers and customers and visit the many Solectron sites around the globe. This perception is shared by the representative from Solectron's supplier, FCI Electronics:

> I still believe that business is about relationships. There are suppliers that have reduced the level of face-to-face interaction, but we've been working hard to get our global business off e-mail. My position is "Let's talk, videoconference, or meet face to face." This is very critical. You win the close deals by having the relationship and knowing your customer's overall business needs. Otherwise, you're always fighting over another penny off for the part. We credit much of our success to our business relationships.

Face-to-face interaction also plays an essential role in the quarterly business reviews that Solectron conducts with its suppliers. The very nature of the supply-chain business—with its narrow margins, intense competition, and tightly choreographed schedules—is stressful. Therefore, face-to-face meetings are better suited to this potentially contentious situation and more conducive to the collaborative problem solving and performance improvement that are the quarterly business review's ultimate objective.

Brocade's management apparently shared Solectron's commitment to face-to-face interaction. In the last chapter we described Joel Sherwood's six-month tenure at the Solectron plant in Columbia, South Carolina, to learn about operations and build relationships that would help him when he returned to Brocade headquarters in Silicon Valley. We also noted that Brocade people frequently spent time on site at the Solectron plant in Penang, and that Jim Sutter often traveled with his Solectron counterpart to strengthen his relationship with him even further.

Learn from Doing

Face-to-face interactions were also the means by which both organizations shared their ideas about how to improve the effectiveness of their joint efforts, as well as to explore opportunities for future collaboration. The Solectron people on the Brocade account met regularly—for example, the account team met about once a week, and Glenn met about once a month with his logistics colleagues and managers. Although these meetings focused primarily on operational issues, they also frequently included discussions of what had been learned from their work with Brocade and how these learnings could be applied to other customers, current and future.

This case also suggests the value of joint learning activities involving representatives from both organizations, as in the forum known as the Hayes Mansion meetings (see Chapter Five). In addition, such events can be a model for mutual learning within companies, to deal with internal collaboration issues and develop collaborative capacity in general. Consider, for example, the potential impact of a forum like the Hayes Mansion meetings involving just Solectron's materials and customer account organizations. Representatives from account management teams for different customers could share their experiences at these meetings and discuss how to adopt and apply this knowledge to new collaborations with other customers. Besides being an ongoing source of innovation for the company as a whole, it would help integrate the two organizations more effectively, supplementing the integration that is currently achieved primarily through the informal point-of-action interactions within the account management teams.

Go for Early Wins

The participants in the Brocade-Solectron collaborations also built relationships and developed mutual trust by going for "early wins"—that is, modest but meaningful successes that could be quickly achieved. That is what Glenn, Matt, and Nigel focused on in the first days of the logistics initiative. They took on the trouble incidents one by one, reducing these specific, well-defined problems from several to about one per week. The metrics that Glenn and

Nigel jointly developed indicated how much was being saved by these early tactical wins. This was a clear demonstration to the skeptics at Brocade of the value of their nascent arrangement with Solectron, and made it easier for Glenn to develop relationships with his new colleagues. This, coupled with his careful reaching out to the skeptics, helped build trust and pave the way for "opening the kimono" even further.

Glenn's success demonstrates the strategic importance of modest early wins in potentially difficult and controversial projects. These successes reinforce the collaborations by building confidence, trust, and momentum. Small successes can quickly add up and help develop readiness for larger, more ambitious efforts. Deep collaboration clearly begins with small steps, especially if these small steps are intentionally designed to achieve quick, modest, but strategically important results.

Conclusion

Table 6.1 shows that Solectron has taken many steps to create the new customer-supplier relationships that are the foundation of its future. The Brocade initiatives illustrate what these new relationships may look like and hint at the benefits that organizations can derive from changing the way they work with other organizations. The actions undertaken by the two companies and their employees to make this partnership work offer a detailed object lesson on how to collaborate effectively across the supply chain, from end to end. Keith McDonald, Solectron's corporate vice president of global accounts, cuts directly to the heart of the matter in his succinct summary of the potential payoff from such efforts: "Open collaboration develops trust and focus, which results in the shortest time to market, and therefore the shortest time to money."

Although the depth of Solectron's collaboration with Brocade is unprecedented in the history of both companies, and in the supply-chain industry as a whole, the company's efforts do not end there, according to David Moezidis: "We must continue to explore new ways to work together [with our customers] to drive [our] future growth." These "new ways" mean new relationships, business models, and even, perhaps, organizations where the boundaries are blurred and constantly shifting to accommodate different partners and unique challenges. These new kinds of organizations will be built around complex collaborations, such as the ones we have described throughout this book.

In the next chapter we will integrate the learnings from all three of our cases and fill in the details of our action framework—that is, the action steps for each of the four phases in the framework. This action framework provides a road map for organizations that want to extend their boundaries, their reach, their competencies, their scope, and therefore the range of challenges and opportunities they can address—in other words, a road map for doing business without boundaries by collaborating across time, distance, organization, and culture.

Chapter Seven

The Action Framework, Part I

From Setting the Stage to Getting Started

The purpose of this chapter and the next one is to develop our action framework by linking all the action steps suggested by the three cases and presented in Tables 2.1, 4.1, and 6.1. This action framework will organize the action steps into a comprehensive, focused plan—describing what should be done, by whom and when—for executing collaborations across time, distance, organization, and culture. (Recall that the overall skeleton of our action framework is presented in Chapter One; see Figure 1.1.)

Our working metaphor for our action framework is jazz: not the tightly orchestrated compositions of Stan Kenton (intricate, predictable, and smooth-flowing) or the free improvisations of Ornette Coleman (unpredictable, chaotic, and, for many, very unsettling) but the music of Charlie Parker and early John Coltrane, characterized by improvisations on clearly stated themes. As in their music, the general flow of broad themes in our action framework suggests approaches and inspires ideas rather than restricting action to narrowly defined boxes. Where we offer specific steps, our intention is to illustrate a concept that readers can interpret in the context of their own organizations' particular needs and circumstances.

Here and in the next chapter, we have added some flesh to this skeleton by extrapolating from the action steps suggested by each of the cases. In doing so, we have taken some liberties in how we interpreted and presented the action steps. We have looked for underlying themes and redefined or elaborated on the action steps to reflect those themes. Sometimes we reshuffled the order of the steps, to reflect what we consider to be a logical but not inflexible sequence, and deconstructed steps to put the pieces into their most appropriate phases. In other instances we went beyond our cases, pulling in action steps from other research, from our own experience, and from the occasional leap of speculation, to provide as complete a picture as possible of what it takes to design and implement a successful complex collaboration. The result is a master list of specific steps, presented in two exhibits in this chapter and two more in the next. The purpose of these four exhibits is to present our interpretation and composite of the action steps from the individual cases and to supplement these action steps, thereby producing a more detailed and comprehensive list that can apply to complex collaborations in general.

Despite the sense of certainty and dogma that such a master list implies, the order of the steps is not fixed, the phases overlap, not all the steps apply in all situations, and not everything that can possibly happen is addressed. In addition, the process described by the action steps is more iterative than linear; some steps may need to be repeated again and again.

We have tried to lay out a detailed and comprehensive "score," but, in keeping with our jazz metaphor, we encourage the "musicians" who follow it to listen to their own muses and improvise their own melodies, coming back to the themes from time to time while keeping the underlying score squarely in mind.

Phase I: Setting the Stage

If this were a perfect world, this is probably where all complex collaborations would begin—that is, with innovative, forward-looking senior executives identifying critical trends and the needs and opportunities created by these trends. These executives would then lead in the development of the appropriate strategy for moving forward and creating the capabilities and conditions for effectively carrying out this strategy.

Of course, this is not a perfect world, and many complex collaborations get started without the stage being set and the appropriate groundwork being laid. Frequently these projects begin more modestly, with an individual project of small scope that can be started and carried out without major changes in existing structures, policies, programs, and practices. In other words, complex collaborations can begin with the action steps of phase II and "bootstrap" higher-level changes as project participants and managers learn what is needed to support these projects and begin to push for appropriate changes in the overall organization.

Therefore, where we have chosen to begin our description of the process is somewhat arbitrary. Regardless of where the process starts, however, the organization eventually has to set the stage for collaboration across boundaries, or even the most innovative and resourceful projects will wither and die. A good place to begin our detailed overview is with what executive management can do to articulate a vision and culture of business without boundaries, develop the potential for fulfilling the vision, create opportunities that can spark this potential into action, and reinforce and support this action so it will happen again. Exhibit 7.1 lists the action steps associated with this "first" phase of our action framework.

Articulate and Promote a Strategic Vision and a Culture of Collaboration

It's not enough for leaders to understand the value of complex collaboration; they also need to convince and inspire others to initiate these collaborations and work hard to help them succeed. One of the first steps in this process is for executive management to articulate and promote a vision of business without boundaries, not just as a short-term response to an immediate need but as a critical element of the organization's long-term strategy. Management has to make it clear in both word and deed that everyone in the organization needs to literally think out of their functional and organizational "boxes" to find potential collaborators to help them solve problems and create opportunities. Organizations and teams are often suspicious of the "boundary spanners" in their midst, that is,

Exhibit 7.1. Phase I Action Steps: Setting the Stage

Articulate and promote a strategic vision and culture of collaboration characterized by mutual respect and a focus on performance

> Speak publicly about it
>
> Write about it
>
> Model the behavior
>
> Celebrate success
>
> Make benefits clear
>
> Examine and reflect on actions that build the desired culture and those that run counter to it
>
> Coach appropriate behavior
>
> Repeat continuously
>
> Implement programs that explicitly promote cross-boundary collaboration

Develop potential through people

> Find the right people, by recruiting and hiring people who have good lateral skills and putting them in positions where these skills can be put to good use
>
> Develop lateral skills throughout the organization, using training programs, job rotation, temporary assignments, and lateral career paths

Create opportunities by building relationships through face-to-face interaction, providing budgetary support for travel, attending meetings, and providing time for employees to build new relationships through networking, and so on

Reinforce and support collaboration over the long term

> Convert potential into action by developing performance assessment and reward systems that focus on collaboration
>
> Support continued, focused action by embedding information and communication systems, performance metrics, standardized contracts, and processes in a collaborative context

those employees who seem to connect as comfortably with people outside their group as they do with those inside. But most now recognize that a narrow, parochial focus is inconsistent with innovation. Not only do organizations and teams need their boundary spanners, they need more of them. Therefore, leaders should encourage employees at all levels to look beyond the boundaries of their teams and organizations for competencies, resources, and perspectives that are not available within these boundaries.

How do they do this? First, they should *take every opportunity to speak publicly about the vision and culture, and do it often*. Repetition works. They should also take every opportunity to *write about it* in annual reports, other company documents and memos and, as demonstrated by the Solectron executives in Chapter Five, in professional and industry journals. But it requires much more than this. Leaders need to *visibly model the behavior* by transcending their functional, organizational, geographical, and cultural boundaries to actively seek appropriate and compatible partners, wherever they may be. They should also *publicly celebrate their successes* when they find them and *make sure that the benefits to be gained from these collaborations are clear and apparent* to everyone. The point of all of this is to encourage others in the organization to help carry out complex collaborations initiated by senior management and to seek out project opportunities on their own initiative. The more people who expand their webs of connections and potential partners, the greater the likelihood of developing frame-breaking collaborations that can remake organizations and even create new industries.

Leaders also need to start building the culture of mutual respect and trust that is the very backbone of the collaborative organization, and to layer on dimensions that stress action, performance, and success. To do this, they should first *examine and reflect on what they are currently doing to build that culture, and what they are doing that may run counter to it*. Then they can engage in activities that reinforce the desired culture and eliminate those behaviors and programs that are inconsistent with it. A critical action step for transforming cultural intentions into reality is *coaching*, especially for reinforcing mutual respect and trust. At Radica, for example, personal feedback and coaching played a very critical role in shaping the culture and the expectations and norms that went along with it. When individuals did not treat others with respect, they heard about it from Bob, Lam, or, later on, from Pat or from someone else in a position of authority. This was usually done privately and with sensitivity, but also firmly. Repeat offenders did not last long at Radica.

These are not one-shot actions, taken early on and then quickly forgotten. All the actions described here for promoting vision, strategy, and culture need to be *repeated continuously* until they become embedded in the very policies and procedures of the organization and in the consciousness and behavior of everyone in it. Even then, they need to be periodically reinforced so that they remain salient and compelling and continue to drive the kind of behavior that fosters collaboration throughout the organization and well beyond.

The last step involved in promoting a collaborative vision, strategy, and culture is for executive management to back up talk and personal action with organizationwide action. Leaders need to literally put their money where their collective mouth is by *implementing programs explicitly designed to promote cross-boundary collaboration*. The John Deere Construction & Forestry Technology program offers an excellent example of this action step. The key elements of these programs include missions, goals, and designs that reflect the vision, strategy, and culture just described. But it also means much more than that, much more than words and encouragement. It also requires significant investment in people and resources to fulfill the vision, execute the strategy, and reinforce the culture. These elements are the focus of the next sets of action steps required to set the stage for specific projects.

Develop Potential Through People

If there were one lesson, and only one lesson, to be learned from the three cases, it would have to be that all collaborations begin with people. That, of course, is obvious. But the qualities and conditions that make people good collaborators, especially the qualities that enable people to cross boundaries and overcome barriers to work with others, are less obvious, and our cases have helped throw some light on this all important issue. This suggests, then, that an important first step is to create the potential for successful complex collaboration by ensuring that people with the skills for successful collaboration are well represented throughout the organization and that they have the opportunity and resources they need to convert that potential into opportunities.

Find the Right People. The first step in creating collaborative potential is for executive management to *recruit and hire people with strong lateral skills* and, whenever possible, *put them into positions where those skills can be put to good use*. As we have seen throughout our cases, this is one of our most important action steps. It's critical not only for staffing broad-based, organizationwide programs, as in the decision at John Deere to assign Mick Sims to run the C&F Tech Program, but also for initiating and conducting the specific projects that will emerge from these and other efforts to set the stage for future projects.

We are not aware of any personality tests specifically designed to assess lateral skills, but there are some promising possibilities in the work of two personnel psychologists, Robert and Joyce Hogan, cofounders of Hogan Assessment Systems, Tulsa, Oklahoma. They have used a combination of three scales from their Hogan Personality Inventory to assess what they refer to as "socio-political intelligence" (Hogan and Hogan, 2002). The scales are "likeability," which measures an individual's empathy, "interpersonal warmth," and the degree to which others are likely to enjoy interacting with the individual; "intellectance," the degree to which the individual is open-minded, tolerant, and "attuned to cultural nuances"; and "adjustment," which measures openness to change, the ability to deal with variety, and "self-absorption" (low "self-absorption" is associated with high levels of "adaptation"). Although these scales have not been widely validated for the specific behaviors, purposes, and contexts we have described throughout this book, the Hogans have successfully used these scales to help select leaders of complex projects. Clearly, there is a convergence between what we describe as "lateral skills" and what they refer to as "socio-political intelligence," and so these scales could be very useful in selecting people for liaison roles as well as for developing collaborative competencies in general throughout the organization. (This description of these scales and their possible relevance to lateral skills is based on a series of personal communications with Robert Hogan.)

Executives, managers, and professional personnel can also use such indicators as experience, history, and past performance to assess and select for lateral skills. Our cases provide some hints about what to look for in considering different people for critical roles in complex collaborative projects. For example, Lam's background and experience made it easy for Bob Davids to recognize his lateral skills and see his potential role in Radica's cross-cultural collaborations; the same was true with Choon Lee Ang and Andrew Gomez at Solectron.

Glenn's previous experience as an importer of African art, while less obvious, also suggests an intriguing possibility. To be a successful importer of art requires a deep immersion in the culture that produces the art. Successful art importers also have to work closely with and appreciate people from very different cultures. Although we have no indication that Glenn's former career was the reason why he was asked to play such a critical liaison role in the Brocade-Solectron logistics initiative, it was pointedly mentioned by several interviewees. His former career was clearly a factor that caught their attention and may have played an implicit role in his selection, at least at some intuitive level in the minds of his managers. Therefore, one of the best indicators of an individual's lateral skills may be his or her demonstrated ease with or previous experience in another culture, whether this means an Asian person working in the West, an engineer working with product designers, or a former academic working in the construction equipment business.

Develop Lateral Skills Throughout the Organization. Finding people with lateral skills is not the only strategy for increasing collaboration within organizations and beyond their borders. *Developing these skills through training programs* is another, complementary approach. Most organizations, especially those with sites in different regions of the world, already have training programs for developing cross-cultural communication skills. This concept does not only apply to groups defined by race, ethnicity, or region, however. All social groups have cultures, including different professions, functional units, and organizations. All these dimensions—race, ethnicity, region, profession, organization—plus others can shape the culture of a particular group. Even different teams performing similar tasks may have different cultures if they are in different organizations or in different regions of the world.

The point is that cross-cultural communication skills can be applied to all kinds of cultural boundaries, not just to those with which we are most familiar. This is what cross-cultural skills training should address—that is, recognizing cultural differences in general, understanding and appreciating these differences, and even embracing these differences because of what they can contribute to our experience and efforts. At its core, this is what we mean by "lateral skills." Therefore, any training program that is successful in developing skills for crossing international or ethnic boundaries could be adapted by interpreting "cross-cultural" more broadly, as communication and collaboration across all boundaries.

Job rotation, temporary assignments, and lateral career paths are also good means of developing cross-cultural competence, especially if employees can progress through jobs in different business units and functions, or through sites with different cultures. Exposure to different cultures will either develop people's ability to collaborate with others from that culture or persuade them that they should look for other lines of work that do not require cross-cultural collaboration. These assignments can also expose people to other perspectives, knowledge bases, and potential colleagues, who in turn can form collaborative pairs around promising project ideas. Cross-functional project teams are another means of exposing people to different perspectives and developing their cross-functional lateral skills.

Create Opportunities by Building Relationships Through Face-to-Face Interaction

The lateral career moves just described have an additional benefit. As individuals move from one site, department, team, or organization to another, they meet other individuals with similar goals but different perspectives. They interact, relationships form, and eventually opportunities emerge from these relationships. The key to the formation of these relationships is face-to-face interaction. Recent research on virtual collaboration has shown that face-to-face interaction is still one of the most important means of building and maintaining relationships and of communicating information and working on shared tasks (see Gibson and Cohen, 2003). Over the last decade, the idea of virtual collaboration has spread throughout the business world, promoted as the cure for skyrocketing travel costs, as the means of linking distant sites and collaborators, and so on. Every day, more and more business leaders, consultants, and writers buy into the seductive vision of individuals interacting with each other via the Internet or videoconferencing technology rather than face to face.

Unfortunately, this fevered interest has tended to distort our perception of how work is actually changing in this era of global enterprise. Recent research and the experiences of many people on virtual teams offer a more nuanced picture of the relative roles of virtual and face-to-face interaction in complex collaboration. Maznevski and Athanassiou (2003, p. 10) succinctly capture the emerging consensus on this issue: "For a virtual team, the single greatest challenge is building relationships . . . [and] it is easier to build strong ties in face-to-face relationships."

Our findings are consistent with this emerging consensus. As our cases demonstrate, face-to-face interaction is essential to building the kind of relationships that are the basis of effective complex collaborations. Therefore, one of the most important steps an orga-nization can take to build these critical relationships is to *provide budgetary support for travel to visit sites, to meet with co-workers in other locations, and to attend meetings and conferences*. And to make sure that boundary-spanning opportunities and capabilities are seeded throughout the organization, support for travel and meetings should not be limited to the uppermost levels of the management hier-archy. Those individuals for whom collaboration will be an every-day activity, and who will ultimately be responsible for making it work, also need to travel to meet, network, and interact face-to-face with their counterparts.

This recommendation flies in the face of recent efforts by most organizations to save money by cutting travel. This can be very shortsighted. As we have seen in our cases, it is better to build rela-tionships before problems arise than to try to get help after the fact, when the problems may be far less manageable. The costs of travel required to solve a problem are probably far greater than the costs involved in building the kind of relationship that can prevent the problem in the first place, or at least mitigate its impact when it cannot be avoided. As Radica's Jeanne Olsen noted (Chapter Four), "Before I had an issue, I had a relationship."

Travel to international conferences, in particular, is a red flag these days for managers and shareholders looking to cut costs any way they can. These trips are often seen as boondoggles and as ex-pensive, wasteful perks for favored executives. But cutting back on these trips can be a counterproductive cost-saving measure that sig-nificantly limits opportunities for future collaboration. Conferences are an excellent venue for networking, and networking is the best way to establish new professional contacts that can lead to poten-tially fruitful interorganizational collaborations.

The kind of assignment and the kind of travel depends on the nature of the boundaries. If a company is interested in developing closer ties with sites in other countries, then that's where critical people should be assigned, to develop culture-specific lateral skills as well as site-specific contacts and connections. If the goal is to expand the network of global suppliers, for example, then key people need to travel to the conferences and meetings where they are most likely to connect with supplier representatives. The guiding principle is that the experience should replicate as closely as possible the boundaries to be crossed—international, interorganizational, cross-functional, or whatever. Furthermore, these opportunities should be available up and down the corporate hierarchy. Because ideas and innovations often emerge from the bottom up and the middle out, organizations need to create opportunities for people at these levels, as well as for their high-level managers, to meet, form relationships, and develop joint projects.

One other resource is needed to help build relationships and develop the ideas that might emerge from these relationships. Boundary spanning and relationship building take time—time to get together, discuss common interests, explore new ideas, and transform these ideas into potential projects. Employees who are constantly under the gun to get work done have little time to network with others and explore new opportunities. This may seem anachronistic in this era of hypercompetition and the pressure it puts on organizations to constantly streamline their operations. At some point, however, organizations have to decide that the marginal benefit of squeezing even more output from their employees is not worth the opportunity costs, and instead they must *provide more time for employees to build new relationships* and try new things. An investment in employee time is an investment in the future.

Reinforce and Support Collaboration over the Long Term

To ensure ongoing and future collaboration, organizations need to develop policies, structures, and systems for supporting boundary-spanning collaborative behavior. These policies, structures, and systems go beyond those typically found in most organizations. Existing ones will at the very least have to be revised and may even have to be completely overhauled or replaced to support the kinds of collaborations we have been talking about throughout this book.

Convert Potential into Action. One of the most important means of encouraging and reinforcing collaborative behavior over the long run is through the organization's *performance assessment and reward system*. This is what transforms collaborative potential—in the form of skills, competencies, and relationships—into successful collaborative behavior and projects. It also helps ensure that these behaviors will endure. The problem is that in most organizations these systems are incompatible with collaboration. What is typically measured is individual performance, and what gets measured is usually what gets rewarded.

True, many organizations in recent years have tried to add dimensions related to teamwork and collaboration to their performance appraisal systems. Because it is still easier to assess individual performance, however, that remains the primary focus for most systems. Besides, traditional notions of individualism, fairness, competition, and protecting "turf" die hard. Therefore, most employees will continue to focus on their own jobs at the expense of others until "the terms of self-interest are changed," in the words of our colleague Susan Mohrman, the noted organizational researcher (personal communication, 2003).

To change the terms of self-interest, organizations have to recognize the strategic importance of collaborative competencies and implement systems for developing these competencies, especially systems for assessing and rewarding collaborative behavior. Until organizations adopt assessment and reward systems that encourage employees to develop their lateral skills, span boundaries, initiate collaborative projects, and work effectively with others, the "collaborative organization" will be little more than a slogan on the wall, and about as effective (see Finegold, Lawler, and Ledford, 1998, for more on the role of competency-based systems in organizational design).

The lack of an appropriate assessment and reward system should not hold up the aggressive pursuit of complex collaboration. It will be easier to overcome natural resistance once projects are under way, preliminary successes are apparent, and collaboration becomes an everyday experience for more and more employees. In addition, there is typically a long lag time between the inception of collaborative behavior and the appearance of project outcomes, particularly in complex projects involving multiple dispersed sites. All of this argues for more modest changes to existing systems, changes that can be implemented quickly. One approach is to assess and reward in-process behavior that, if continued, will eventually lead to project success—for example, helping others, treating people with respect, and consistently demonstrating sensitivity to cultural differences. Going for early wins, as suggested by the Solectron case, and rewarding these wins is another way to keep participants motivated through the many months, or even years, required to bring these long-drawn-out, complex projects to a successful conclusion (see Lawler, 1999, for more discussion of reward systems that support teams and teamwork).

Support Continued, Focused Action.   Effective, ongoing collaboration requires an infrastructure to support appropriate behavior and processes. The Solectron case illustrates the critical elements of this infrastructure as well as the collaborative context—the expectations, norms, and intentions—that makes this infrastructure something more than just an inanimate collection of disparate systems and practices. The elements of this collaborative infrastructure include *information and communication systems*, and *standardized contracts, practices and performance metrics*.

The realm of communication and information systems provides a good example of what we mean by a collaborative context. Typically, the expression "systems" and its counterpart, "technology" conjure up images of monitors, keyboards, and boxes—that is, "hardware"—and the software they contain or can access via the Internet. But our use of the term "systems" conveys much more than that, encompassing not just the hardware and software but the business strategy, norms, and expectations within which the technology is embedded.

The Radica case illustrates this point well, especially the Bass Fishin' game project. With relatively rudimentary communications technology (primarily fax and phone), the company was able to transcend international boundaries and execute a major transformation of its product line and a turnaround in its fortunes in a very short period. Radica did this with a clear idea of how to use the technology it had and with clear expectations about when and what to communicate and how quickly to respond to communications from others. Just as important were the company's norms emphasizing mutual respect and cultural sensitivity in all Radica's communications, whether face-to-face interactions or messages transmitted by phone, fax, or, later on, e-mail. That is what made Radica's collaborations work—integrated systems of strategies, norms, and technology, not just the technology alone. A similar point can be made about the use of information technologies like the global data warehouse at Solectron. Its power as a tool for complex collaboration derived not just from its ability to provide a comprehensive and integrated look at critical data but also from Solectron's strategic decision to share some of this information with its customers and suppliers.

We do not mean to suggest that the technology itself is unimportant. Information and knowledge are the essence of work in the new global economy, and so the technology for integrating and working with this knowledge across boundaries is the key to collaboration in the twenty-first century. But the technology alone is not enough. It creates the potential, but it doesn't ensure that the potential will be realized or channeled in the most productive directions. What makes the technology and other elements of the collaborative infrastructure useful in places like Radica and Solectron are the collaborative processes in which they are embedded and the strategies, norms, and expectations that guide their use. These are the factors that add real value to the infrastructure and make it come alive as a vehicle for collaboration and as a foundation for business without boundaries.

Summary

The steps just described are not one-shot actions; they need to be repeated continuously. In fact, it's probably misleading to even characterize them as steps, which implies a well-defined beginning and end, rather than as ongoing activities that are always necessary and always relevant, regardless of the organization's mission and the nature of its tasks and projects. Furthermore, the organization-level changes just described do not necessarily have to be in place for projects to get started. If they did, few projects would get very far. The structures, systems, and culture for supporting collaboration over the long run will arise from what is learned from actual projects, whether successful or not. That does not mean, however, that building this capability has to wait until after several projects have been conducted. Building capability should be part of the ongoing collaborative process. The projects will reveal the needs. As projects unfold, participants will learn what their organizations can do to support these and future projects and complex collaborations in general. This process can start as soon as there are learnings to consider.

Phase II: Getting Started with Specific Projects

Phase I deals with creating readiness for complex collaborations throughout the organization. Now we begin our discussion of specific projects—in this section, how to get them started, and in Chapter Eight, how to carry them out. There are three ways projects can get started: from the top down; from the bottom up/middle out, when senior management has set the stage in phase I; and from the bottom up/middle out, when senior management has not set the stage. Our three cases illustrate each of the three situations. As we saw in the cases, all three approaches can work, at least to some extent, but the action steps for making them work are somewhat different. Each approach and its respective action steps is summarized in Exhibit 7.2 and discussed more fully in the following passages.

Exhibit 7.2. Phase II Action Steps: Getting Started with Specific Projects

Starting projects from the top down

1. Identify need
2. Provide high-level structure, and search for compatible partners if the collaboration is interorganizational
3. Create liaison roles (considering single person versus separate liaisons, defining responsibility and autonomy, and including lateral integration as a primary responsibility)
4. Put people with lateral skills in these roles
5. Provide them with opportunities to create collaborative pairs through face-to-face interaction
6. Collaborative pair begins building project team by bringing in others as needed
7. Project team develops proposals and presents them to management
8. Management reaffirms support for project and provides resources
9. Create collaborative pairs between project sponsors

Starting projects from the bottom up and middle out

1. People with lateral skills form collaborative pairs to explore project ideas and compatibility (corresponds to steps 4 and 5 in a top-down project, but modified to reflect different origin)
2. Collaborative pairs bring in others as needed (similar to step 6 in a top-down project); if senior management has not adequately set the stage, more effort may be required to get others involved
3. Project team develops proposals and "sells" them to management (similar to step 7 in a top-down project except that effort will be required to sell the project, and even more will be required if senior management has not adequately set the stage)
4. Management affirms support for project and provides resources (similar to step 8 in a top-down project)
5. Create collaborative pairs between project sponsors (similar to step 9 in a top-down project)

Starting Projects from the Top Down

The Radica case is the only clear example among our cases of a complex collaboration actually initiated by someone at or near the very top of the organization. Bob Davids recognized the need for a new direction for the company and initiated the Bass Fishin' game project to take Radica down this new path. He also made the initial decisions concerning how to structure the project by defining, partitioning, and allocating the key tasks among the Dallas, Hong Kong, and southern China sites. In addition, he understood how important it was to have someone serve as a liaison to integrate the sites, and he recognized that Lam's experience and lateral skills made him the ideal person to fill this critical role. Bob and Lam then put together the team to develop the new game.

Bob's example illustrates several key action steps that all senior managers can follow to get projects started. Radica was atypical at the time—for example, the company was small and informal enough for Bob to be closely involved throughout most of the project. Therefore, we have drawn on the other cases and on our own experience to build on Bob's example and identify action steps for initiating complex collaborations from the top down. Except where noted, all the steps are actions taken by senior management. Since the action steps listed here are roughly sequential, we have numbered them in order.

1. Identify the Need.   In our cases, the best example of this step was offered by Bob Davids, who identified the need for a radically new product that could save the company. Another example can be seen in the Solectron case, with the company's senior management deciding to pursue closer collaborations with customers and suppliers. These examples illustrate that a need can be very specific, such as developing a new product with specific features and getting it to market in time for Christmas, or very general, such as setting a new strategic direction, as in the Solectron case. Regardless of what kind of need is identified, it should drive everything else, including the nature of the complex collaboration, the people involved, and the actions they take.

2. Provide High-Level Structure. In the case of an interorganizational project, this would involve finding partners with shared goals, complementary capabilities, and compatible cultures, as well as general guidelines about the limits of authority for project participants, governance structures, and so on. For a complex collaboration within a single organization, like the Bass Fishin' game project, it may involve designing the basic task structure just as Bob Davids did when he decided to design the product in Dallas, engineer it in Hong Kong, and manufacture it in China.

3. Create Liaison Roles. There are at least three issues to be addressed in this step. The first issue is whether this role can be adequately filled by just one person or whether the situation requires separate liaisons for each of the teams, organizations, or sites involved in the collaboration. This is not a decision that has to be set in stone for the duration of the project; it can be modified later on by the project team in consultation with the senior managers who set the project in motion. The second issue involves defining the role to include operational responsibility for getting the project going as well as the autonomy that the people in these roles will need to fulfill their responsibilities. The third issue is that whoever is responsible for defining and supporting these roles should ensure that the primary responsibilities involve lateral integration and coordination across the collaborating teams, organizations, and sites. If the project is not too complex, the role can include additional responsibilities not directly related to liaison functions. Nevertheless, too many additional responsibilities, especially if these other responsibilities are important enough to compete for the liaisons' time and attention, can undermine the purpose of the role, the effectiveness of the people in these roles, and ultimately the success of the project.

4. Place People with Well-Developed Lateral Skills in These Roles. Other factors in addition to lateral skills need to be considered in selecting people for these all-important roles. Liaisons should also have substantive knowledge appropriate to the project. Political factors may be an issue as well; for example, in the case of a single liaison linking two sites, it helps if the person in this role is known and has credibility at both sites. Balancing all the considerations is key, but lateral skills should be weighted heavily in choosing the right people for these roles.

5. Give Liaison People Opportunities and Support for Face-to-Face Interaction. This step is necessary for building good relationships among the liaisons in the different teams, sites, or organizations involved in the collaboration—in other words, for *creating collaborative pairs*. These interactions should not only be task-based but should also include the opportunity for informal social interaction. The latter helps each person learn about the larger context and circumstances of the others' work. Knowing the whole person makes it easier to understand and accept someone else's perspectives and behavior. We should also note that if there are more than two organizations involved, the interactions and relationships may involve more than pairs, possibly even a small integrating team made up of the liaisons from all the collaborating sites.

With this action step, the locus of action now shifts to the collaborative pair (or integrating team).

6. Collaborative Pair Begins Building Project Team. The liaisons, working with management, identify potential team members to help with the project. The criteria for selection should be similar to those described for the liaison roles except that substantive skills should be weighted more heavily here. Lateral skills are important for everyone on the project team, however, especially if different functions, sites, and organizations are to be represented on the team.

7. The Project Team, Facilitated by the Liaisons, Generates Whatever Is Required by Management to Approve the Project (for Example, a Proposal, a Prospectus, and So On). The proposal should be as formal as possible—that is, written, comprehensive, unambiguous, and well defined—especially if the project is very complex. Management should also be involved in this process, working collaboratively with the project team to ensure that the proposed project is closely aligned with business needs. Management's involvement can also ensure that the proposal provides as compelling a rationale as possible for the project and that it includes all that is needed for the project to be approved. The locus of action now shifts back to management.

8. Management Reaffirms Support, Assigns a Sponsor, and Provides Resources. This is different from the general support and resource management provided in phase I because these resources are allocated specifically for this project.

9. Create Collaborative Pairs Between Project Sponsors. Before the project is actually launched, the executive sponsors from each of the organizations involved in the project should create an executive-level collaborating pair or integrating team. The purpose of this pair (or team) is to oversee the project, initiate and coordinate action that requires higher-level authority, and provide an escalation path for conflicts that cannot be resolved by those involved in day-to-day project tasks.

Starting Projects from the Bottom Up and Middle Out

Many complex collaborations bubble up from lower levels of the organization. In fact, some even argue that this is where innovation should begin, from the bottom up and the middle out (see, for example, Ciborra, 2002). Individuals do not always have to be told by management what new initiatives to pursue. Sometimes they just need to be inspired by management's vision and provided with the opportunity to think out of the "boxes" defined by the boundaries of their teams and organizations. Then they can come up with the ideas themselves—by trying to figure out how to do their tasks more effectively, by thinking of new uses for new technologies, or by coming up with ideas for new products or services in collaboration with others in the normal course of their work. That was how the Solectron-Brocade logistics initiative was started.

The stage had already been set at Solectron by executive management when Jim Molzon visited Matt Taylor at Brocade to help work out a service issue between the two companies. (Jim, of course, as a vice president, was hardly working from the bottom up, but there were several layers of hierarchy above him, and he was not acting on specific directions from management at those levels. His initiative might more accurately be described as starting from the middle out, or maybe even from the upper middle out.) Solectron's new strategic direction, emphasizing closer collaboration with customers and suppliers, had planted the seed, and so even though Jim was not visiting Brocade for the explicit purpose of exploring this possibility, he saw an opportunity and seized it. Brocade was fertile ground for this mutual exploration because its executive management had a similar interest in innovation, new directions, and close collaboration with appropriate partners. Both Jim and Matt had good lateral skills and a similar entrepreneurial bent, and so it wasn't long before the idea for the logistics initiative emerged from their interactions and they formed an informal collaborative pair. They each picked someone to work on the operational details of this new partnership and assigned these people to work together. This collaborative pairing between Glenn and Nigel is what enabled the initiative to get off to such a good start.

From this example we can see that the action steps for this approach are somewhat different from what happens when the project is initiated and driven at the highest levels of the organization. Instead of the project creating the collaborative pair—that is, instead of senior executives choosing the liaisons—the collaborative pair creates the project. The pairing happens not by intention but by serendipity influenced in part by high-level vision and strategy. Management's vision defines the issues of importance to the organizations and thereby helps the collaborators identify ideas worth pursuing.

Because the project emerges from the interactions between open-minded people looking for compatible opportunities, project ideas are not assigned, and people are not designated to pursue these ideas. Therefore, steps 1 through 3 under the top-down approach are not relevant here. Instead, the process begins with people who have good lateral skills taking advantage of the opportunity for face-to-face interaction provided by leaders through their action steps in phase I. As these individuals explore projects of mutual interest with their counterparts on other teams or in other organizations, they build relationships; that is, they create collaborative pairs. These steps correspond roughly to steps 4 and 5 under the top-down approach except that the ideas and interactions emerge from the initiative of the people involved rather than being handed down to them from management.

As their ideas develop, they bring in others to help develop the ideas further (similar to step 6 under the top-down approach), and they generate whatever is required (a charter, a proposal, a prospectus, and so on) to gain management's support for the project (step 7 in the top-down approach). Even though management has already signaled, through its vision and strategy, its general support for such projects, each of the partners in a collaborative pair may still have to sell the specific project idea to their managers. No doubt there will be other proposals competing for management's attention and support, and so getting the go-ahead is not a slam dunk, regardless of how consistent the project is with the intent and spirit of the leaders' vision. The recommendation we made earlier about getting management involved in this step is even more crucial here because the project was not initiated by management and has probably received little of management's input or guidance up to this point. As in step 8 in the top-down approach, management needs to affirm its support for the project, assign an executive sponsor, and provide resources before the project can move forward. The last step is also similar to the top-down approach (see step 9)—that is, creating collaborative pairs between project sponsors, to oversee the project and deal with issues that require higher-level authority, integration, and resources.

When Senior Management Does Not Set the Stage. The John Deere case provides another example of the bottom-up/middle-out approach, but with an important difference. Myra Holt of ABC and Don Garnet of Central Minnesota College (CMC) were the emergent, informal collaborative pair that got the C&F Tech Program going at CMC. As in the Solectron case, neither Myra nor Don had a specific directive from their bosses to partner with each other to develop the new program. They knew each other from previous contacts, and Don had already been involved with an earlier, unsuccessful program run by ABC. Also as in the Solectron case, they had good lateral skills and a mutual concern for the issue the program was designed to address.

The key difference between the two cases is that the executive management of ABC had not set the stage as proactively, intentionally, and explicitly as did the leadership at Solectron. Of course, ABC was interested in new ideas and initiatives, but deep collaboration with other organizations was not as central to ABC's strategy as it was to Solectron's, nor had ABC done as much to promote and support this idea throughout the company. Therefore, Myra needed to find an executive sponsor before the idea for a new program could be transformed into an actual project. She found that sponsor in the newly hired executive vice president, who not only provided symbolic support but also urged the other members of the executive team to support the new program and "leaned" on the dealers to get their support for the project. Last but far from least was the access to resources he provided, in the form of time for Myra and then Joan Jackson to devote to the project, in addition to the budget to support their efforts.

These circumstances call for a somewhat different approach. Since senior managers will have provided little explicit guidance about what kinds of projects they are willing to support, more effort on the part of the project initiators will be required to get other people involved (step 6) and sell the project idea to their managers (step 7).

Convincing managers to visibly support the project (step 8) and work collaboratively with their counterparts in the other organizations (step 9) will also be more challenging in these circumstances. This situation is the most difficult of all. The projects are not initiated by management, nor has management set the stage to help get them going, but sometimes there is no alternative but to take the initiative and work like hell to get the support needed to get the project started. This is not an ideal situation, but, as we saw in the CMC project, it can work, at least in terms of getting projects started. But it doesn't bode well for the long term unless early results convince senior management to become more proactive in nurturing the project as well as in creating fertile soil for growing future complex collaborations.

Conclusion

These three cases illustrate what is needed to get complex collaborations started: promoting and supporting a vision of collaboration across boundaries, putting the right people in the right place, giving them the opportunity to connect with their counterparts in other teams and organizations, and then, when appropriate, seizing the opportunities that arise from these serendipitous connections. We now come to the transition from the preliminary phases, leading up to the formal go-ahead for the project, to the heart of the process itself: working on the project tasks. That is the focus of the next chapter.

Chapter Eight

The Action Framework, Part II

From Creating the Infrastructure to Doing the Work

In this, the last chapter of the book, we present the action steps for the last two phases of our action framework. In the first two phases, our focus was on the steps leading up to the project; in the third and fourth phases, we deal with the actual conduct of the project itself, from the first tasks undertaken by the team members and their managers to the completion of the project. By the end of this chapter, we will have compiled a comprehensive list of steps for collaborating across time, distance, organization and culture.

As we argued earlier, this list of steps is not an instruction manual to be slavishly followed, without a thought to the purpose of each step and the principles underlying it. Therefore, at the end of this chapter we will revisit the two threads introduced in Chapter One—the threads of "relationships" and "structure"—to gain a deeper understanding of the action framework and its nature, purposes, and intent. By the end of this chapter, it will be clear that the detailed descriptions and analyses of the three cases presented in the preceding chapters have provided an in-depth understanding of these two threads and the connection between them. Most readers will then be able to generate the steps on their own and improvise new ones, only occasionally referring to the "score" of our action framework to remind themselves of where they are going and how to get there.

Phase III: Creating the Infrastructure

This is the first phase that deals specifically with the conduct of the project. The focus in this phase is on laying the groundwork for the project by creating structures and processes to help participants understand everyone's roles and responsibilities, execute tasks, make decisions, manage the project, and work together with the other members of their teams. The phase after this also deals with the conduct of the project, but the emphasis shifts from laying the groundwork to doing the actual project tasks. There is some of each in both phases, but the relative emphasis does change from this phase to the next. The action steps for this phase are presented in Exhibit 8.1.

Build and Design the Project Team

Building and designing the project team actually begins in phase II, when the members of the collaborative pair bring in others to help develop the project idea into a proposal to be presented to management for their formal support (see Chapter Seven). After management has approved the project, allocated a budget, and assigned an executive sponsor, it is time to transform this informal, ad hoc collection of individuals into an actual project team with a well-defined mission and charter.

The people who worked on the proposal will make up the core of this project team. They may not have enough skill, knowledge, and time, however, to carry out such a complex project. They will need help. The first step in finding this help requires *identifying the high-level work tasks* (step 1 in Exhibit 8.1). This does not mean the actual detailed tasks that need to be executed to fulfill the project goal, but rather the broad, general task areas, so that *new members can be added who have the competencies and skills* needed to supplement the competencies already represented on the team (step 2 in Exhibit 8.1). These new members will be drawn from the different units, sites, and organizations participating in the project. New members can also be added for political purposes, to represent key constituencies that can exert their influence in important ways (for example, by providing resources and impacting the eventual fate of the project). Although lateral skills may not be as critical for all

Exhibit 8.1. Phase III Action Steps: Creating the Infrastructure

Build and design the project team

1. Identify high-level work tasks
2. Add new members with needed expertise and skills
3. Learn more about the conceptual and applied knowledge that will guide the design of the infrastructure and tasks

Create structure and process—the overall structure (4-6), expectations about collaborative behavior and process (7-9), identification of resource needs (10-12), and development of plans for the transition to doing the work (13-14)

4. Define adaptive goals and objectives, and develop performance metrics
5. Design governance and authority structures for representation, simplicity, and clarity (for example, differentiate between advisers and doers; define decision-making processes)
6. Formally define roles, tasks, responsibilities, and relationships (including leadership roles and approach); facilitate autonomy, but be directive as necessary
7. Identify communication needs (schedule frequent meetings; create and maintain links between project participants and the organizations and teams they represent)
8. Establish understandings and ground rules for communication, information sharing, and about actively recruiting partners' employees
9. Develop a charter to codify roles, communication needs, ground rules for communication, information sharing, active recruitment, and so on
10. Identify information needs (the more complex the project, the greater the needs)
11. Identify other resource needs
12. Present resource needs to management
13. Develop a plan for project tasks
14. Develop plans for learning

team members as they are for those in liaison roles, they are still important and should serve as a selection criterion for all team members. This criterion would be in addition to those related to task expertise and skills and to whether team members represent key stakeholders or constituencies. This is similar to actions taken in phase II (see Chapter Seven) except that here it applies to the larger project team rather than just to those brought in by the collaborative pair to help with the proposal.

With new members added and broad tasks identified, the project team is almost ready to start creating the infrastructure to support its collaborations throughout the project. Before the team members begin, however, they need to *learn more about the infrastructure that they will design, the tasks that they will soon undertake, and the conceptual and applied knowledge that should guide this effort* (step 3 in Exhibit 8.1). Mohrman and Cummings (1989, p. 36) describe this step as it applies to their model for organizational self-design (their focus is somewhat different, but the basic ideas are the same): "When organizations or their subunits begin self[-]design, they must prepare themselves for activities that differ substantially from daily routines. This preliminary stage provides basic knowledge needed to get started. Without such information, the design process may be ill-informed and superficial."

For our purposes, this training and education should include, among other topics, knowledge about collaborative processes, team development, project management, and the information technology that will be used. An especially important element of this training is cross-cultural communication skills. This training is different from the more generic training described for phase I. The training we propose here would build on that foundation but would be tailored to the project by focusing on the specific boundaries to be crossed. For example, if a project required international collaboration, then the training would target the cultural boundaries associated with the cultures of the regions involved in the collaboration. If the primary challenge were cross-functional collaboration, as with a new-product development team involving representatives from engineering, manufacturing, and marketing, then the program could focus on familiarizing all participants with the languages, paradigms, and knowledge bases of the different functions represented on the team.

The training should also include basic information on organization design, especially as it relates to infrastructure and process design issues that participants will soon face (for example, questions about how to build norms and shape behavior in ways that are consistent with the desired culture and project goals). Participants may also need to supplement their knowledge about the substantive focus of the project (as with questions that involve the particular product, program, or process they are charged with developing). Finally, as noted by Mohrman and Cummings (1989, p. 37), this is not just a one-time thing but instead "continues throughout the process as participants become more sophisticated and enthusiastic about designing." In fact, we would argue that the best time to offer this knowledge is when the team is actually dealing with particular issues. For example, information about different approaches to leadership, to decision making, and to governance structures would be most helpful as the team is actually dealing with these issues.

Create Structure and Process

This project team will be different from the typical project team. Because we are talking about complex collaborations that can involve multiple organizations in different locations, the boundaries of the overall team may be ill defined, and the membership may be more fluid than usual. Therefore, designing and facilitating this project team will be especially difficult. To reduce the potential chaos, one of the first orders of business for this project team will be to create the structure that will be needed for managing, conducting, and supporting the project.

This leads us to the heart of phase III: creating the actual infrastructure for the project. We have partitioned the action steps into four groups:

A. The first group (steps 4–6 in Exhibit 8.1) deals with the overall governance and structure of the project. Several of the issues addressed by these three action steps are similar to what might be found on an organization chart, plus the job descriptions that go along with the positions identified on the chart.

B. The second group (steps 7–9 in Exhibit 8.1) includes the expectations and understandings that will guide the behavior of the people involved in the project as well as how they interact and communicate with each other and with external stakeholders.

C. The third group (steps 10–12 in Exhibit 8.1) has to do with the information, systems, and other resources that the project team needs to do its work.

D. The fourth group (steps 13–14 in Exhibit 8.1) deals with the transition into the last phase of the action framework, that of actually doing the tasks that are the focus of the project.

Overall Structure of the Project.   This group of steps has to do with defining goals and objectives, designing governance and authority structures, and defining roles, tasks, responsibilities, and relationships.

Define Goals and Objectives.   The first step in this category (step 4 in Exhibit 8.1) is to define the goals and objectives of the project and identify how progress and performance will be assessed. Management should play a significant role in this step. Organizational leaders will most likely define the broad goals or mission of the project—for example, the development of a new product with specific features to be on the market by a specific date. Within the boundaries defined by management, however, the project team may have considerable leeway in defining objectives and developing performance measures. As we learned in the Solectron case, project teams should consider adopting initial goals that are modest and can be quickly achieved, or at least adopt goals that can be modified as conditions change, as the John Deere case suggests.

Design Governance and Authority Structures. After that, or possibly at about the same time, the project team should design the project governance and authority structures (step 5 in Exhibit 8.1). Decisions about governance and authority are some of the most important issues that the participants will have to address.

There are actually two dimensions to this step. The first has to do with governance and authority structures within the project team and deals with such issues as how the project will be led and managed, who will fill the leadership roles, and how decisions will be made. The second dimension has to do with the relationship between the project's governance and authority structures and the organizational or interorganizational structures within which the project is embedded. This dimension includes, for example, processes for reviewing and implementing project decisions in addition to escalation paths for resolving conflicts that cannot be resolved within the project team. The distinction is important because management needs to be closely involved in decisions concerning the interface between project governance and the organizational authority structures that provide the context for the project. Except for questions that deal with the project team's leadership, which we will discuss shortly, management does not and probably should not be involved in decisions concerning the internal processes and structure of the project team.

The criteria for guiding the design of both internal and interface governance structures are the same: the structures and processes should be fair, clear, and unambiguous; should be as simple as possible; and should provide adequate representation for all the teams and organizations involved in the collaboration. Distinguishing between advisers and doers, as in the John Deere projects, is a good way to deal with these criteria.

Define Roles, Tasks, Responsibilities, and Relationships. A related step (step 6 in Exhibit 8.1) is to formally define roles, tasks, responsibilities, and relationships. Part of this step—defining the role of the leader in particular—is relevant to the issue of governance and authority structures. In other words, how should this role be filled? By an individual, or should it be shared? For a fixed period, or should the leader's term be open-ended? What are the responsibilities of the person(s) in this role, and what are the expectations for how those responsibilities will be carried out? Our cases are especially illustrative with respect to this last issue. All three cases strongly suggest that the most desirable approach is a facilitative one that provides as much autonomy as possible to team members as long as everyone also understands and accepts the need for a more directive approach as circumstances may require.

Management may need to be involved in the decision about who fills leadership roles, but management should tread carefully in dealing with this issue. At the very least, management should discuss and consult with the project team about who should lead the team, but joint decisions are best. In most cases, management will reserve the right to veto unacceptable choices.

The project team should also revisit the issue of project liaisons. The people who were instrumental in getting the project started, and who therefore initially served as liaisons for the project, may not be the most appropriate people to serve in this role going forward. They may be better suited for the role of project leader(s). Although it may be possible to serve as both liaison and leader in the early stages of a project, the demands of both roles may be too much for one person later on, especially if a project is very complex, such as one involving virtual collaboration among multiple teams in different organizations and countries.

After goals, it is difficult to say which of the other issues—governance and authority structures, roles, tasks, responsibilities, and relationships—should be addressed first, which second, and so on, because they are so closely linked. Our view is that these are not distinct, sequential steps but instead define a domain of critical issues that probably should be addressed together. For example, governance and authority structures have significant implications for roles, and vice versa. Any discussion of one should probably include the other, and there should be some going back and forth between them, and some adaptation of decisions about each one, until all the pieces fit together. So, even though we have numbered the steps sequentially, the intent of our recommendations is to ensure that all the critical pieces get addressed, not to dictate their order.

Before we move on to the next set of action steps, we should note that the project team should adapt and use existing organizational structures whenever possible, as was done in the Solectron-Brocade initiatives, rather than create new ones from scratch. This will not only save work but also make it easier to integrate the project with the processes and structures of the organizations involved in the project.

Expectations About Collaborative Behavior and Process. After the project team has created the basic project infrastructure, an infrastructure that will probably be modified once the project progresses far enough to reveal flaws and suggest improvements, the next group of steps has to do with identifying communication needs, establishing ground rules for communication, and developing a charter to codify agreements about communication needs and ground rules.

Identify Communication Needs. The first task here is to identify communication needs (step 7 in Exhibit 8.1), both internally (among members of the project team) and externally (among individual team members and key people on the team or in the organization, including direct managers, project sponsors, and others). The issues to be addressed include what needs to be communicated, to whom, how, and how often. Our cases suggest that it is important to schedule frequent meetings, especially in the early stages, and to try to provide opportunities for face-to-face interaction.

This step is especially important for maintaining the links between project participants and the collaborative entities—teams, departments, organizations—they represent. Participants can sometimes "go native" in the kinds of boundary-spanning projects we have talked about throughout this book; that is, they can lose touch with their constituents if they do not make a special effort to keep in touch with them over the course of a project. It's only natural for people to draw closer together as they work intently on highly interdependent tasks. The problem is that the very same forces that pull people together within project teams can pull them away from their colleagues, co-workers, and managers still "at home" in their organizations and teams.

This did not appear to be a significant problem in any of our cases. Most participants, especially those in critical linking roles, made special efforts to keep connected with the units they represented. Glenn, for example, regularly met with his managers at Solectron and communicated with his department every week. Nevertheless, we have seen this problem come up in other projects, and it usually has serious consequences. Therefore, in this action step we strongly recommend that project team members explicitly address the issue of how to maintain linkages with the teams, units, or organizations they represent by using regularly scheduled communications, meetings, and so on. (It is hard to overlook a meeting that has been posted on a public, widely available schedule, whereas good intentions about regular communication, if they have not been formalized through meetings or other means, are relatively easy to forget.)

The role definitions described earlier can also help to avoid or at least significantly mitigate this problem if the role definitions include regular communication and other linking activities between project teams and the collaborative entities they represent. Getting people's input and keeping them informed will not only contribute to the quality of the outcomes but also help ensure continued support from all parties throughout the project.

Establish Ground Rules. Along with expectations about communication frequency, means, and intentions, the project team needs to establish communication ground rules (step 8 in Exhibit 8.1) early in the project. These ground rules should deal with such issues as e-mail etiquette, cultural sensitivity, how quickly to respond to communications from others, information sharing, and behavior consistent with mutual respect and trust. By agreeing on these expectations and making them explicit at the earliest stages, the project team creates the basis for norms that will guide behavior from the project's first days through its frequently difficult midpoints (Gersick, 1988) and on to its eventual conclusion. The project team needs to move from words to deeds by deciding what constitutes appropriate behavior and determining what will be done to deal with inappropriate behavior when it occurs. As the project unfolds, new issues will emerge, and the limitations of the abstract expectations defined early in the project will be revealed. Once the participants have experienced the heat of battle and the fog of war, the project team should plan on revisiting these expectations from time to time in the process of doing the work.

Other expectations, understandings, and ground rules should also be addressed early on. For example, Solectron's understanding that Brocade would not try to lure Glenn away with attractive job offers, and the "gentleman's agreement" between ABC and Northland not to actively recruit each other's students, suggests another issue for discussion. Complex collaborations among multiple organizations can expose participants to job opportunities offered by other organizations involved in a project. The key is to develop understandings about respect for organizational boundaries as demonstrated by not intentionally trying to lure employees away from a partner. The project team should carefully craft these understandings to make sure that they do not run afoul of laws barring unfair constraints on individuals' access to job opportunities. Reaching mutual understandings about sharing information is another important action step for creating effective interorganizational collaborations.

Develop a Charter. The next action step is to pull all these agreements together and codify them in a formal charter, contract, or other form of written document (step 9 in Exhibit 8.1). This is the "bible" for the project, the touchstone to which the project team members can always return to remind themselves of important agreements, to resolve disputes, and to focus action. Just as important as the document itself are the candid discussions and deliberations that produce it. Without a requirement to put understandings and agreements in writing, team members may be tempted to leave important issues hanging, with a vague belief that everyone agrees on them—a belief that may not survive the inevitable conflicts and disagreements that arise in difficult projects.

Resource Needs. The next group of steps has to do with identifying information needs, identifying other resource needs, and presenting these needs to management.

Identify Information Needs. Information needs—including data, applications, and systems—now have to be identified for the project (step 10 in Exhibit 8.1). Many years ago Jay Galbraith, in his groundbreaking book on organization design, noted that "the greater the task uncertainty, the greater the amount of information that must be processed among decision makers during task execution in order to achieve a given level of performance" (Galbraith, 1973, p. 4). In other words, the more complex the project, the more information and information technology will be needed to manage its complexity.

We can see this relationship in action by comparing the Solectron case with the John Deere case. The former is more complex—more organizations (suppliers and customers), different kinds of relationships (suppliers versus customers), dispersed sites, greater time pressures, and outcomes that are more critical to the companies involved. Therefore, the use of information and technology is much greater in the Solectron case than in the John Deere case. We see a similar relationship when we compare the two projects at Radica. The earlier, simpler Bass Fishin' game project was able to get by with fax machines and telephones, whereas the controller projects had access to more advanced and complex technologies such as e-mail and 3-D design systems.

Identify Other Resource Needs. At this point, the project team should also identify other resource needs (step 11 in Exhibit 8.1). These needs may include physical space, training, and access to others who have specific expertise.

Present Resource Needs to Management. Requests for these resources, or at least a budget for acquiring them, can be presented to the project sponsors (step 12 in Exhibit 8.1) for their approval at the same time as the information and technology needs. In addition, the project team should identify and present other ways (politically, symbolically, and so on) for organizational leaders to support the project. If all these requests are presented together, project sponsors and other members of the management team can get a realistic and comprehensive picture of what the project team needs in order to carry out a successful project.

Transition to Doing the Work. The final action steps in phase III are concerned with developing a plan for executing the project tasks and plans for learning from these tasks.

Develop a Plan for Executing Project Tasks. Developing a plan for a complex collaborative project (step 13 in Exhibit 8.1) is no different from developing plans for any other kind of project. This plan should cover such issues as the tasks to be done, who is responsible for each task, the sequences, dependencies, and critical paths that link these tasks, and the deliverables and timelines.

Develop Plans for Learning. Developing plans for learning (step 14 in Exhibit 8.1) involves learning from doing the tasks and then making revisions on the basis of what has been learned. Good project plans, by definition, include plans for learning. Some of the learning has to do with the nature of the tasks themselves—for example, monitoring results to see if some tasks need to be added, dropped, or revised. What is different about a complex collaboration is what can be learned from engaging in the collaborative processes themselves and the improvements that can be made in the collaborative infrastructure on the basis of these learnings.

The distinction between learning from project tasks and learning from collaborative processes is central to our action framework, and so it deserves further emphasis and clarification. A new-product development project involving separate teams in different countries, such as the Bass Fishin' game project at Radica, will generate two kinds of learnings as team members work on the project. One kind of learning concerns the new product they are developing. This may involve such issues as whether the product can be built at a cost that enables the company to make a satisfactory profit, and whether the product's features will attract potential customers. These questions and issues have to do with the project goals and the tasks that have to be executed in the pursuit of these goals—in other words, with the process of doing the work. The other kind of learning has to do with how well people collaborate in doing the work. The focus is on the collaborative structures and processes used to accomplish the work, not on the work tasks themselves. For example, are the means of communication adequate? Do people use them appropriately? Do they treat each other with respect? If they don't, why not? These are the kinds of issues and the kinds of learning we are talking about in this action step. We refer to these as the "collaboration tasks," to distinguish them from the other kind, the "work tasks" or "project tasks." The work tasks are the primary subject of phase IV of our action framework, but we will see that they are intrinsically bound up with the collaboration tasks and that they provide another opportunity for further development of the collaboration infrastructure.

Phase IV: Doing the Work

The focus of this phase is on executing projects tasks, learning while doing so, and revising tasks, processes, and structures accordingly. The groundwork for these activities is laid in phase III, when the project and learning plans are developed. As before, the line of demarcation between this and the preceding phase is somewhat arbitrary and fuzzy. A case could be made for waiting until the collaboration infrastructure has been completed before starting with project tasks, but the reality may require a quite different approach. The natural urge is to get on with it and begin working on the project. This is understandable and probably irresistible, and so the overlap is inevitable. It probably won't affect the project adversely as long as the urge to start working on the project tasks does not get in the way of laying the foundation that will ensure that these tasks are done right. It may even help to interleave some collaboration and work tasks early on, to keep participants motivated and create a sense of progress and momentum. Therefore, many of the action steps described in this section could just as easily have been presented in the previous section, and vice versa. These action steps are summarized in Exhibit 8.2.

Exhibit 8.2. Phase IV Action Steps: Doing the Work

Execute project plan and work tasks

Execute work tasks

Further develop and strengthen relationships through face-to-face interaction and other media

Promote, model, and coach mindfulness and cross-cultural sensitivity

Execute learning plan

Periodically monitor performance of project tasks, evaluate, and reflect on results

Monitor, evaluate, and reflect on collaboration structure and processes

Revise goals, plans, structures, and processes

Revise project work tasks and collaboration structure and process

Create expectations about flexibility and change

Disseminate learnings to high-level decision makers

Execute Project Plan and Work Tasks

This set of action steps involves what most people would consider the real "meat" of the project—*executing those work tasks* specifically focused on achieving the goals of the project. The process of carrying out these tasks also provides an opportunity for *further development of the collaborative infrastructure and processes*. To execute the project tasks, team members will have to coordinate their tasks and communicate with each other and with others outside the team. As they do this, they will be able to strengthen their relationships through face-to-face contact and other media, and they will be able to develop new relationships. They and their leaders will also have the opportunity to put the abstract ground rules and expectations they developed in phase III to the test of actual use. By *promoting, modeling, and coaching mindfulness and cross-cultural sensitivity*, they will convert these ground rules into internalized norms that can intuitively guide desired behavior. The key to accomplishing these secondary but nevertheless important objectives can be found in the next action step.

Execute the Learning Plans

The project/learning plans developed in phase III should include steps for *periodically monitoring the performance of project tasks and plans* and for *reflecting on and evaluating the results*. This should be done collectively; that is, all team members and others associated with the project should share ideas and experiences and be involved in discussions about improvements.

The learning plans should also include similar activities for *monitoring, evaluating, and reflecting on the collaboration structures and processes* developed in phase III, to see how they can be improved. This also should be done collectively. The point of these action steps is to make sure that the collaboration infrastructure and processes are not taken for granted. Deliberate attention must be paid to these issues in order for the project to achieve high levels of success.

Revise Goals, Plans, Structures, and Processes

As we saw in the John Deere case, conditions change, and large, complex, long-term projects rarely turn out as planned. If goals and plans do not change in response to this dynamic environment, a complex collaboration will not only fail to achieve its original goals but will also fail to achieve anything else that could ultimately justify the considerable effort, resources, and cost that went into the project. Therefore, the project team should *revise the project's work tasks and its collaboration structure and processes*, if such revision is appropriate, on the basis of the learnings gained in the previous step. Throughout this process—in fact, throughout the entire project—project leaders, sponsors, and others should work to *create expectations about flexibility and change* among team members and other stakeholders.

Disseminate Learnings to High-Level Decision Makers

The purpose of the last action step is to leverage the learnings from individual projects into large-scale organizational change—into the kinds of structures, policies, and practices, described in phase I, that are needed to support collaboration throughout the organization and beyond and to set the stage for future projects. To accomplish this, *project team leaders should disseminate to high-level decision makers what the team has learned concerning the organization-level structures, policies, programs, and processes needed to support complex collaboration*. This not only will be important for the current project but also may help the leaders of the organization develop a more collaborative organization in general.

The Hayes Mansion meetings conducted by Solectron and Brocade are a good model for this last action step. Because these meetings involved senior-level managers as well as those involved in day-to-day collaborations, dissemination of learnings was almost guaranteed. Learnings about how to develop and manage complex collaborations were directly passed on from those involved in these collaborations to the managers responsible for creating the kind of organization that would encourage, enable, and support future boundary-spanning collaborations such as these.

This step also provides a fitting end to this book, spiraling back as it does to the first phase of our action framework, with one very significant change. Organizations that undertake such projects and are genuinely committed to collaboration in all its forms are changed by the experience. Each project sets the stage for a new round of complex collaborations that are built on knowledge gained from the projects that came before. In other words, with each project, the organization incrementally builds the capacity for collaboration across time, distance, organization, and culture.

Recap and Conclusion

The purpose of this book is to help executives, managers, consultants, and others create successful collaborations among dispersed teams, diverse cultures, and multiple organizations. With the action framework presented in this chapter and Chapter Seven, teams and organizations can cast a wider net, and they can cast it farther, to get the people, resources, and knowledge needed to conduct business without boundaries. This framework is not the result of an intellectual exercise, nor is it based on deductions and rationales drawn from abstract, academic principles. Instead, the framework is based on the actual experiences of several organizations and individuals wrestling with—and, for the most part, overcoming—the challenges they faced in their own attempts to collaborate across boundaries.

The three cases we have presented are varied, and—on the surface, at least—the experiences in each case seem quite different. But our analysis of each case reveals consistent findings across all three, suggesting action steps that can be applied universally to all kinds of complex collaborations, regardless of their purposes, their forms, or the conditions in which they operate. Readers can use the action steps summarized in Tables 2.1, 4.1, and 6.1 and in Exhibits 7.1, 7.2,

8.1 and 8.2 as the basis for action checklists tailored to the specific systems and circumstances of their own projects and organizations (see Duarte and Snyder, 2001, for excellent examples of checklists for related purposes). In addition, many of the behaviors and actions we have described can be incorporated into performance appraisal systems or used as learning objectives for training modules. Their use in this way can help institutionalize collaborative behavior and incorporate it into the very DNA of the organization.

Readers may reasonably ask why we went to so much trouble to describe and analyze these cases in such detail. Our reason for presenting the cases that way was to anchor the action steps in reality, so that our readers could see the details and nuances of what people actually did. For example, our recounting of Bob David's role in shaping Radica's culture and norms says a lot more about how to accomplish this than any abstract description or statement could ever have done, regardless of how thorough and well thought-out it might have been. Our hope is that the cases presented in this book will enable our readers to take away a deep, intrinsic, almost intuitive understanding of the challenges of complex collaboration and how to deal with them.

Here, in the final pages of the book, we would like to push this understanding a bit farther, even beyond the action framework presented here and in Chapter Seven. Admittedly, the framework may be daunting, with so many steps spread over four phases. Therefore, in these last few paragraphs, we offer a metaprinciple that captures the essence of the action framework and integrates the action steps within it. For the most part, the action steps are essentially specific manifestations of this metaprinciple. This metaprinciple is much easier to keep in mind, and it may be all that is needed in many situations and projects. It is our hope that once the metaprinciple is internalized and deeply grasped, the specific action steps to be taken will easily follow, and that they will flow naturally from the convergence between the logic of the principle and the particular conditions of each project.

The broad outlines of this metaprinciple were presented in Chapter One, although we did not refer to it as such. We did refer to the two threads that weave through our action steps and help tie them together. One thread represents the "soft" side of a complex collaboration—that is, the people, their relationships, and how they work together. The other thread represents the structuring elements that support the collaboration by helping to focus action, inform decisions, and buffer against distraction. These two threads are related and inseparable. Structure supports collaboration, and collaboration produces structure. Both threads are needed to weave the fabric of complex collaborations; without both, the garments will fall apart. These are the fundamental truths that underlie our action framework and our perspective on how to make complex collaborations work.

The two threads represent the yin and yang of our metaprinciple—the interdependence of structure and relationships. The synergy between the two can be summarized by two broad points:

1. *Collaborations start with relationships*. Therefore, the first steps are to help these relationships develop, by initiating specific projects or by "enabling serendipity"—that is, creating conditions that enable these relationships to form spontaneously around common interests, which in time may evolve into joint projects.

2. *Relationships are the axis for launching a formal, more extensive effort*. The first task in this effort is to use the relationship to create the structure that will help the participants focus more effectively on their collaborations and tasks.

This metaprinciple and our summary of it capture the spirit, if not the details, of our action framework. By internalizing this metaprinciple, using it as a mind-set, and referring as necessary to the action framework for details, managers and others should be able to design any type of complex collaboration, regardless of its form, type, or circumstances. To return to the jazz metaphor with which we started, this metaprinciple provides the theme; the action framework provides the score. Readers, like jazz musicians, can use the theme to improvise on the framework and create collaborations that transcend all boundaries to produce deeply fulfilling performances.

References

Carbone, J. "Purchasing Strategy: Solectron Prepares for the Upturn." *Purchasing Magazine*, October 24, 2003, n.p. Reprinted in *Solectron Inside*, January-March 2003, pp. 4–6.

Ciborra, C. *The Labyrinths of Information: Challenging the Wisdom of Systems*. New York: Oxford University Press, 2002.

DePalma, V. "Another Crossroads." *Electronic Packaging and Production*, February 2002, n.p.

Dougherty, D. "Interpretative Barriers to Successful Product Innovation in Large Firms." *Organizational Science*, 1992, 3(2), 179–202.

Duarte, D. L., and Snyder, N. T. *Mastering Virtual Teams: Strategies, Tools, and Techniques That Succeed* (2nd ed.). San Francisco: Jossey-Bass, 2001.

Erez, M., and Earley, P. C. *Culture, Self-Identity, and Work*. New York: Oxford University Press, 1995.

Finegold, D., Lawler, E. E. III, and Ledford, G. E. "Organizing for Competencies and Capabilities: Bridging from Strategy to Effectiveness." In S. A. Mohrman, J. R. Galbraith, E. E. Lawler III, and Associates (eds.), *Tomorrow's Organizations: Crafting Winning Capabilities in a Dynamic World*. San Francisco: Jossey-Bass, 1998.

Flanigan, J. "A Recovery High on Efficiency, Low on Jobs." *Los Angeles Times*, August 24, 2003, pp. C-1, C-5.

Flanigan, J. "'Offshoring' Can Create Jobs, Too." *Los Angeles Times*, February 29, 2004, pp. C-1, C5.

Galbraith, J. R. *Designing Complex Organizations*. Belmont, Calif.: Addison-Wesley, 1973.

Gersick, C. J. "Time and Transition in Work Teams: Toward a New Model of Group Development." *Academy of Management Journal*, 1988, 31, 9–41.

Gibson, C. B., and Cohen, S. G. (eds.). *Virtual Teams That Work: Creating Conditions for Virtual Team Effectiveness*. San Francisco: Jossey-Bass, 2003.

Hogan, R., and Hogan, J. "Leadership and Socio-Political Intelligence." In R. E. Riggio, S. E. Murphy, and F. J. Piarozzolo (eds.), *Multiple Intelligences and Leadership*. San Francisco: Jossey-Bass, 2002.

Klein, K. J., and Ralls, R. S. "The Organizational Dynamics of Computerized Technology Implementation: A Review of the Empirical Literature." In L. R. Gomez-Mejia and M. Lawless (eds.), *Advances in Global High Technology Management*, vol. 5A. Greenwich, Conn: JAI Press, 1995.

Lawler, E. E. III. "Creating Effective Pay Systems for Teams." In E. Sundstrom and Associates (eds.), *Supporting Work Team Effectiveness: Best Management Practices for Fostering High Performance*. San Francisco: Jossey-Bass, 1999.

Mankin, D., Cohen, S. G., and Bikson, T. K. *Teams and Technology: Fulfilling the Promise of the New Organization*. Boston: Harvard Business School Press, 1996.

Maznevski, M. L., and Athanassiou, N. A. "Designing the Knowledge-Management Infrastructure for Virtual Teams: Building and Using Social Networks and Social Capital." In C. B. Gibson and S. G. Cohen (eds.), *Virtual Teams That Work: Creating Conditions for Virtual Team Effectiveness*. San Francisco: Jossey-Bass, 2003.

McGinty, M. "Plenty of Machines, but Who Will Keep Them Running?" *Construction Equipment Distribution*, 1999, 65(10), 25–30.

Mohrman, S. A., Cohen, S. G., and Mohrman, A. M., Jr. *Designing Team-Based Organizations: New Forms for Knowledge Work*. San Francisco: Jossey-Bass, 1995.

Mohrman, S. A., and Cummings, T. G. *Self-Designing Organizations: How to Create High Performance*. Belmont, Calif.: Addison-Wesley, 1989.

Pava, C. *Managing New Office Technology: An Organizational Strategy*. New York: Free Press, 1983.

Solectron Corporation. *This Is More. More Speed. More Value. More Possibilities*. Annual report. Milpitas, Calif.: Solectron Corporation, 2002.

Sproul, L., and Kiesler, S. *Connections: New Ways of Working in the Networked Organization*. Cambridge, Mass.: MIT Press, 1991.

Townsend, R. *Up the Organization*. New York: Knopf, 1970.

Townsend, R. *Further Up the Organization*. New York: Knopf, 1984.

Index